Penguin Education

Penguin Modern Psy
Occupational and Org
Editor: Peter Warr

Learning and Change in Groups
Arthur Blumberg and Robert T. Golembiewski

Arthur Blumberg and Robert T. Golembiewski

Learning and Change in Groups

Penguin Books

Penguin Books Ltd,
Harmondsworth, Middlesex, England
Penguin Books Inc.,
7110 Ambassador Road, Baltimore, Maryland 21207, U.S.A.
Penguin Books Australia Ltd,
Ringwood, Victoria, Australia
Penguin Books Canada Ltd,
41 Steelcase Road West, Markham, Ontario, Canada
Penguin Books (N.Z.) Ltd,
182–190 Wairau Road, Auckland 10, New Zealand

First published 1976
Copyright © Arthur Blumberg and Robert T. Golembiewski, 1976

Printed in the United States of America by
The Colonial Press, Inc., Clinton, Massachusetts 01510
Set in Monotype Times

Contents

Preface

Well over a dozen books and many times that number of journal and magazine articles have been published in recent years having to do with sensitivity training, T-groups, or encounter groups. The content range of these publications has been wide, including almost zealous advocacy of experiential group learning, academic criticism, and reports of sophisticated research.

The focus of this book is on the experiential learning group as a vehicle for learning about personal, interpersonal. and group relations in work and educational environments. We acknowledge the personal therapeutic purposes for which learning groups are used – indeed, we discuss that issue – but our thrust throughout the volume is on the dynamics of training and learning, not therapy. The latter we leave to clinicians.

The intent of this book is to explain and not to advocate. While both of us are group practitioners and researchers, our purpose is not to urge a group learning experience on the reader. Rather, we offer a broad perspective of the group field so that the uncertainty that may exist regarding T-groups, for example, may be at least partially cleared. The book ought to be useful, as well, to people who have participated in a learning group. It may help them view and analyse their experience in retrospect.

The length of the book precludes a more detailed analysis of many of the issues that it raises. For the reader who is interested in pursuing the inquiry, we suggest two much more comprehensive texts. These are R. T. GOLEMBIEWSKI and A. BLUMBERG, *Sensitivity Training and the Laboratory Approach: Readings about Concepts and Applications*, 2nd edition, 1973, and R. T. GOLEMBIEWSKI, *Renewing Organizations*, 1972, both published by F. E. Peacock Publishers, Itasca, Illinois, U.S.A.

Things rarely start from zero. Such is the present case. The original version of Chapters 3–8 appeared in A. BLUMBERG, *Sensitivity Training: Processes, Problems and Applications*, a monograph published by the Syracuse University Series in Continuing Education in 1971. We are indebted to Dr Doris Chertow, editor of the series, for permission to make use of the monograph in the way we have. We are also in the debt of our academic colleagues and other writers whose words we have used and upon whose ideas we hope we have built.

ARTHUR BLUMBERG
Syracuse, New York
ROBERT T. GOLEMBIEWSKI
Athens, Georgia

1 Demands for Learning, Change, and Choice in Groups

Shakespeare captured much of the essence of the human condition in his dramatic: 'To be, or not to be . . . ?' In a few words, he raised the universal spectre we both dread and delight in. He focused on three central dynamics of what it means to be human: to learn, to change, and to choose what we will be even if it is only a choice to remain as we are.

Prior to the late 1940s, a person became consciously engaged in a formal process of self-learning, changing, or choosing usually through individual psychotherapy or counselling. Those who did usually came from the upper socio-economic strata of society. And for ample reason, for the process was costly and time consuming.

This situation has changed radically. A 'group movement' devoted to individual learning and change has spread rapidly through Western society, from its roots in developments at the Tavistock Institute in London and the National Training Laboratories in the United States. This movement, which takes its theoretical basis from the behavioural sciences and psychotherapy, has brought, or in many cases sold, the opportunity for deliberate self-learning experiences to a much wider spectrum of the population. If one seeks a better understanding of self and others, it is no longer necessary to engage a therapist. One need only go to a week-end or a week-long group experience. The costs are not exorbitant and the time can be spared by most people. And it seems reasonable to suspect that for great numbers who attend, the promise is fulfilled, at least in part. They tend to report exciting and meaningful experiences and probably serve as the best salesmen of groups to their friends and colleagues.

Though it is clearly not a purely American phenomenon, the

American scene has witnessed a much wider proliferation of institutionalized group learning than Western Europe or Great Britain. The first sentence of a recent voluminous report of research on experiential learning in groups is: 'Today's American is fairly likely to come face to face with the question of membership in an encounter group.' (Lieberman, Yalom and Miles, 1973, p. 3). Why this is so has not, to our knowledge, been investigated.

Indeed, the question of whether or not to 'go grouping' is likely to be less momentous than choosing what kind of an experiential group to do it in, for the possibilities are numerous and varied. As Yalom (1970, pp. vii–viii) notes with particular reference to the United States:

... a recent survey of representative groups, run in the Northern California Bay area, discloses a bewildering array of approaches: psychoanalytic groups, psychodrama groups, crisis groups, Synanon, Recovery, Inc., Alcoholics Anonymous, marital couples groups, marathon encounter groups, family therapy groups, traditional T-groups, personal growth T-groups, nude therapy groups, multi-media groups, non-verbal sensory awareness groups, transactional analysis groups, and Gestalt therapy groups. Many of these are designated as therapy groups; others straddle the blurred boundary between personal growth and therapy.

Our concern is with groups and group learning wherever it is found. Our purpose is to paint a broad yet detailed picture of what a learning group is, how it develops, and what may happen to people as a result of their participation.

The demand for group experiences

This chapter looks at the rapid spread of group experiences often known as T-groups, encounter groups, or sensitivity training; it then discusses six major explanations for the explosive growth of this movement. The inquiry first briefly evaluates research on the outcomes of group training experiences. It then explores some of the arguments advanced to account for the growth of group learning.

The proliferation of attempts at innovative group learning is different from the new teaching programmes recently introduced into formal education settings. For the most part such things as 'new maths' have found their way into curricula and, after a period of time, they have either been dropped or bastardized by the sub-culture of the schools. The result is that there is an illusion of change in the schools but very little change of substance (Sarason, 1971). The group movement is different. Rather than being integrated into and diluted by existing organizations, it appears to have developed an identity of its own. It is self-sustaining, and seems to generate its own impetus for growth.

Research as a motivator for seeking membership

There are two certainties about group experiences. First, no single factor can account for the massive demand for group experiences coming from individuals, groups, and organizations. Secondly, that demand is not due to many people doing what research says is good for them.

Research on individual change as a result of intensive group experience is only beginning and is inconclusive in many important particulars. Chapters 9 and 10 will look at research in detail. Briefly, the results attributed to group experiences vary depending on who is asked, and when. The most thorough study of the effects of an encounter group was made by Lieberman, Yalom and Miles (1973). They found that about 60 percent of the college student participants afterwards described their experience as having been beneficial. However, the leaders of the groups were much more optimistic about the numbers who had benefited. They estimated that 90 percent of the participants experienced 'some change', and about one third 'substantial change'. The timing of data-collecting, however, is critical. A follow-up study some six months after training found significant changes in perhaps 10 or 20 percent of the participants who earlier cited beneficial aspects of the training. Overall, this noteworthy proportion of participants '... were less enthusiastic about the positive change they perceived previously' (Lieberman, Yalom and Miles, 1973, p. 128).

Overall, Lieberman and his associates conclude that

'... encounter groups show a modest positive impact, an impact much less than has been portrayed by their supporters and an impact significantly lower than the participants' view of their own change would lead one to assume' (Lieberman, Yalom and Miles, 1973, p. 130).

In an extensive review of T-group research, Campbell and Dunnette (1968) come to a similar conclusion about the results of T-group training experiences, particularly as they are related to change in managerial behaviour. While pointing to what appear to be self-reports of positive personal learning from training, they also note that little behavioural change is transferred into work relationships. Further, with regard to internal criteria of change – self-perceptions, for example – Campbell and Dunnette (1968, p. 99) point out that: 'It still cannot be said with any certainty whether T-groups lead to greater or lesser changes in self-perceptions than any other types of group experience, the simple passage of time, or the mere act of filling out a self-description questionnaire (more than one time).'

All such research is easy enough to fault, and easier to interpret in various ways. Thus there is no compelling reason to expect that the Stanford undergraduates studied by Lieberman and his associates are representative of the large number of aggressive seekers after group experiences. Moreover, important changes are reported in even the two studies summarized above, which certainly cannot be accused of over-enthusiasm for group training. Most participants report changes in values, attitudes, and even self-image. In the Lieberman study, for example, participants reported they became more oriented towards growth and change. Moreover, self-images also tended to improve – participants saw themselves as more tolerant and understanding, and as having developed a greater congruence between the ideal self and the perceived self. These are powerful effects for any brief experience.

Despite such considerations, one conclusion remains: the proliferation of group experiences cannot be explained on the basis of hard data. This is not to say that productive learning to do with attitudes and skills does not result from the group. But these results are insufficient to account for the huge numbers of people who want to attend groups. Clearly, other things are operating. Were these 'other things' not at work to create both pushes and pulls for people to engage in intensive group learning situations, the movement would probably have died. But it waxes strong. Hence the need to seek other explanations for the robustness of the group movement, four of which are sketched below.

Making up an emotional deficit by a group experience

The search for these 'other things' leads initially to a different level of analysis. This level of analysis deals with the more or less intangible, yet crucial, quality of the culture of the small group. One need only to listen to participants to get a flavour of it. They do speak of specific things they have learned – to listen better, or to test assumptions about other people. But the essential emotional bond that participants have for the group seems to derive from categories of experience other than learning and practising specific interpersonal skills. These are related to the internal substance and dynamics of the group, and include:

* experiencing a rare sense of community;
* becoming close to people in an unusually intense way;
* being able to share their warmth with another person, particularly of the same sex and especially between men;
* becoming free to reveal themselves as people;
* developing a sense of their own personal worth that might have been previously lacking.

For reasons that are not altogether clear, human relations training groups of whatever specific orientation develop a culture that most participants find exhilarating. A positive group experience leaves people with a sense that they have not really been alive before, that they have experienced too little of the richness around them, that their emotional engines run only fitfully and inefficiently.

In these senses, the group experience at once highlights and satisfies a significant emotional deficiency, even if only for the short period of time that the group exists. It is quite possibly true that most people are unaware of any such lack prior to their participation. No matter. One does not have to seek something in order to find it, or even know that it has been lost.

The making up of an emotional deficit may be a large factor in the continuing demand for learning, change, and some realistic sense of choice through group experiences. Not every participant becomes enamoured of his group and what it means to his emotional life. But many do, and apparently they serve as good enough salesmen for their friends and co-workers to keep demand rising. This line of argument does not suggest that learning new skills is unimportant. But the motivation to seek group experiences must go far deeper than participants reporting outcomes such as 'I learned to listen to people'. People must need that experience in very deep, human ways.

The importance of this need is suggested by Rogers (1970). His concept of an emotional deficit implies crucial things missing in a person's day-to-day life – in work, college, church, family or what have you:

> It is a hunger for relationships which are close and real; in which feelings and emotions can be spontaneously expressed without first being carefully censored or bottled up; where deep experiences – disappointments and joys – can be shared; where new ways of behaving can be risked and tried out; where, in a word, he approaches the state where all is known and all accepted, and thus further growth becomes possible. (Rogers, 1970, p. 11).

For Rogers, then, seeking a group experience is not only akin to satisfying a hunger. Rather the goal is positive personal growth.

Group experience as a social oasis

Yalom's (1970) position regarding the function of group learning is similar to Rogers', though he expresses it in terms of a respite from the façade-building nature of competitive American culture rather than 'hungering'. At the root of Yalom's argument is the idea that once a person has become successful in the eyes of his peers, he strives, at all cost, to maintain that image of success. Feelings of inadequacy are repressed and the individual is constantly on guard against letting uncertainty become public. This process is a costly one, often preventing a person from engaging in new and creative ventures if they are risky.

Experiential groups, according to Yalom, provide an opportunity for a person to escape, if only temporarily, from this need to maintain a façade:

All accoutrements which in the outside world symbolize success and normality are deposited at the door of the T-group. Individuals are no longer rewarded for their material success, for their hierarchical position, for their unruffled aplomb, for their efficiency, or for their expertise in their area of specialization; instead they are exposed to the totally different values of the T-group, in which they are rewarded for interpersonal honesty and for the disclosure of self-doubts and weaknesses. (Yalom, 1970, pp. 351-2).

Yalom's description of the T-group as a 'social oasis' makes sense from his analysis. For many people, apparently, it has become important to find a place with other like-minded people where, for a short period of time, the outside world and its demands take second place.

Pilgrimage as the essence of group experience

Back's (1972, 1973) analysis of the widespread demand for experiential group learning provides a different perspective. His view is both historical and anthropological, in contrast to Rogers' focus on the psychological. Back (1972) suggests that man has always had a need for pilgrimage. The trek of great numbers of people to personal growth centres is only a modern example of a broadly human urge, or perhaps even some primitive animalistic drive. Lemming-like, masses of people are somehow driven to a common experience that they do not really understand but can at best only rationalize.

The sense of pilgrimage at the heart of seeking for group experiences can be a kind of clever put-down. Back tries to make it much more, by perceptive speculations about guiding motives for pilgrimages, which have typically involved a sacred belief, a religion, or an ideology. The group movement does have religious overtones for many people. There is no deity, of course, but some deep sense of sacredness or even mysticism often surrounds the group experience. If a religious experience involves a deep communion with one's fellow man, there is little doubt that some – perhaps even many – people have arrived at just such a communion in a T-group. In such cases, a kind of sacredness would attach to the group, and participation would be seen as a desirable and sought-after cleansing experience.

The spiritual or religious analogy can be extended. The ideology of the group pilgrimage places an extremely high value on individual and interpersonal authenticity, to destroy the hypocrisy of modern-day life. Many interpersonal and social problems result from the dishonest façades forced on people when they have to play organizational roles instead of behaving like 'human beings' in an honest, forthright manner. Authenticity requires that one learn or relearn how to behave so that the façades disappear and one becomes free to be oneself. Group experience shows that such relearning is both necessary and possible.

Whatever may be said of pilgrimages, the ideology of authenticity has proved a powerful one over the last decade or so. It has had a particular appeal for the young, who have reacted against what they see to be appalling cases of political and intellectual dishonesty. 'Doing your own thing' has been perhaps the most vigorous expression of this ideology.

For his anthropological analysis, Back (1973) uses Bernstein's (1970) concepts of group and grid systems of organization and communication. He explains: '"Group" refers to a conscious division of societies into sub-sets that stress the importance of membership and the maintenance of strong boundaries in all aspects of social life, with clear distinctions between in- and out-groups' (Back, 1973, p. 10). The 'grid' variable, on the other hand, focuses attention on conditions in which relationships are developed and maintained by a concern with people irrespective of status, social class, and so forth.

These distinctions generate some useful analysis. In 'high group' conditions, an individual gains identity through particular group memberships. Group memberships define personhood. In 'high grid' conditions the focus is on the development of identity through interpersonal relationships and interaction, rather than on the basis of group membership.

Back suggests that the experiential group movement is a reaction against what he sees to be the low group/low grid condition of Western society. On the one hand, many traditional group memberships have been diluted or destroyed – whether they derive from ethnic, regional, small community, or similar influences. This is a 'low group' condition. On the other hand, Back also notes that today's society is also 'low grid': '. . . all relationships are formalized, rationalized, professionalized, depending not on the person, but on his skill or knowledge' (Back, 1973, p. 11). The combination is not satisfying for people. In very simple terms, the problem is one of a frustrating search for lasting identity in a world that changes ever faster.

For Back the sensitivity training group represents a low group/high grid condition. It provides an opportunity for people to replenish that part of their lives that is somehow found lacking in daily life. But Back emphasizes that a low group/high grid condition is inherently unstable, and that the T-group is a temporary thing. The intensive group experience is therefore as much problem as it is solution. It can be even worse if, for example, it gives people a taste of what they cannot hope to duplicate in the world outside the group.

The turbulence of post-industrial society

Back says directly and Rogers implies, then, that any reasonable answer to why thousands of people seek out intensive group experiences must recognize the turbulence of our post-industrial society. The turbulence has had its effects on large organizations, universities and schools, the family, and other groups, as well as on the attitudes and behaviour of individuals. It has, for example, created a sort of 'temporariness' (Bennis and Slater, 1968) that will, in all likelihood, become a permanent characteristic of the Western world. The signs are everywhere. One third of the people in the United States do not live in the same home or stay in the same job from one year to the next (Packard, 1972). And if they are in the same work situation, the chances are that their job relationships will change because of reorganization, or because temporary problem-solving groups working on specific projects are dissolved.

This temporariness raises two major issues. In one sense, temporariness makes necessary quick and constructive responses to the increased instability of life. For many people an encounter or personal growth centre is a 'cultural island' where an individual can take stock, test self out with others, and try to develop a new picture of social reality. This stepping out of the world, as it were, enables the individual to step purposefully back into it. Ideally, the individual will be better able to manage self and to respond effectively, or at least confidently, when confronted with bewildering demands for new and temporary social relationships. This promise of a chance to renew oneself so as to cope better with the fast-moving world is certainly a powerful drawing card.

The second issue related to the increased temporariness of life has to do less with the ability to cope emotionally, and more with a person's ability to be effective as he moves from one transient situation to another. Very pressing challenges are posed to a person who confronts each new group and realizes that its life may be a short one. At the crux of the challenge is the question: 'How do I, as an individual, make better use of myself here so that I get my needs satisfied, and also can contribute to the overall effectiveness of the group?'

On this second issue, again, the group movement holds out some promise of resolution, even though – or, perhaps, especially since – the group experience is also temporary. A participant has to make the most out of it during its life. Often for the first time, the participant learns how much can be accomplished in a short time, how even strangers can work together effectively. The experience can form a new set of expectations about life.

These possibilities – of glimpsing a new social order and of becoming more skilled in interpersonal and group relationships – are attractive ones, particularly to people in large organizations. Hence group training experiences – often sponsored by business and industrial organizations – continue to have ample applicants, many of whom come away satisfied.

The effects of social turbulence seem to be most overtly manifest in the behaviour of students on college and university campuses. And it is on the campus that group experiences seem to be most prevalent, with such experiences often available in cafeteria-like profusion. For many students, no doubt, the cultural anchors that gave security and direction to their parents no longer exist; for most students, certainly, these anchors are much weaker than they once were. For instance, the nuclear family is not the source of security it was.

The consequences of such lack of roots are difficult to characterize. Many students have turned inward. The underlying notion is that security and, perhaps, peace which once may have existed in the world 'out there', can now only be found within the self. Encounter groups provide the opportunity to share intimately with like-minded people, to disregard power and authority, and to be a 'human being'. The encounter provides what formal education often neglects – a chance to relate to others and to oneself in ways that are different and sometimes exciting, and with a new sense of intimacy.

Affluence and the turning to groups

Another factor is the unparalleled affluence in Western society, particularly in the United States, that followed the Second World War. There are small-group learning proponents in some under-developed countries, such as India, but their goals are almost entirely instrumental – directed at managerial and organizational development. Only in highly-industrialized and affluent societies, apparently, can the luxury of personal growth and development be provided for a wide spectrum of the population, and not just a select few. Nowhere else are the time and the money – and perhaps the need – available in the quantity necessary.

There are three related features in this greater concern for personal growth and development in the affluent West. Affluence has spread suddenly to a larger proportion of the population. In addition, a far larger proportion of the population seeks aid in coping with a broader range of concerns of the 'healthy' person, as distinguished from the concerns of the ill associated with very lengthy and costly procedures, for example, psychoanalysis. Now it is possible, or so the promotional literature of many growth centres tells us, to achieve insight into one's character, to become more sensitive and more personally integrated, by spending a week-end or a week with like-minded people undergoing a group experience at reasonable cost.

Two concluding points

There are two last points to be made in attempting to understand the demand for, and hence the acceptance and institutionalization of, individual learning and change through groups. Firstly, there has always been a strong element of science associated with the group movement, and its leading exponents are respected behavioural scientists. Promotional brochures of even the shakiest of growth centres list the academic qualifications of their staff. The general image, then, is of a scientifically-developed learning technology, which also just happens to have an appeal to the public. Indeed, there is a great deal of academic concern with groups, and much legitimate research has been conducted on the group and on results of group training. Nevertheless, it is true that the academic, scientific ploy is used extensively to oversell group experiences as a palliative for all that ails man.

The second point is more speculative and harder to document. It has to do with the manner in which social and educational innovations grow and take hold in Western culture, particularly in the United States. The group movement was born and grew *outside* formal educational institutions, even though its founders have been educators of one type or another. It was new both in philosophy and methodology. Had it been introduced into schools and colleges at the outset, it might well have died at birth. The kinds of learning that groups focus on – emotional and behavioural – tend to be antithetical to the intellectual biases of formal schooling. When T-groups do find their way into the curriculum, even now, they are usually listed with rather vague academic-sounding titles so as to enhance their intellectual respectability.

In summary, then, any attempt to understand the experiential group movement and the demands for learning and change that individuals place on it, must take into consideration a wide variety of interacting forces. These forces are psychological, sociological, anthropological, and economic. No specific weights are assigned to the several forces discussed here, for that no doubt would reveal more of our biases than it would reflect reality.

2 Basic Concepts of Learning and Change in Groups

This chapter describes the processes whereby an individual learns and changes in an experiential learning group. The task is a complex one, and the term 'processes' is central to that complexity. What is learned in a group is a function of the specific kind of interaction that takes place – the 'what' outcomes are intimately related to 'how' processes. .

So complex are such processes that most theorists avoided them. Most learning theorists do not take process differences into account; Lewin is an exception. Quite early on, he '. . . set himself squarely in favour of a psychological analysis of the *actual situation* and against what he called *accomplishment* factors' (Hilgard, 1948, p. 212). Rather than focusing attention on the result of learning, Lewin was interested in the behavioural processes occurring while learning was taking place. It was more important to discover what was happening to an individual as he was learning to use a typewriter, for instance, than it was to measure how many words he typed a minute.

However, while Lewin's notions about behaviour and its causation have recently influenced many learning theorists, they do not constitute, nor apparently were they intended to be, a psychology of learning. The best that can be done here, then, is to direct the reader to an eclectic conceptual arena. The arena is not complete; nor do its various components constitute a whole. The overall effect, however, is useful.

Experiential learning

Much that is central in the processes of group learning derives from their experiential character. Much claptrap also derives from the term 'experiential'.

First consider some characteristic claptrap. Much education

at all levels today is caught up in the anti-intellectual mystique of experience. The only learning that is worthwhile is that which is 'relevant', goes the common refrain, and relevance can only be obtained through personal experience. Thus, particularly among the young, the knowledge and experience of *others* tends to be devalued.

However, experience does not necessarily lead to productive learning nor, indeed, to any learning. Merely to put people in groups so that they may experience each other can have good results, no results, or damaging results. After all, a person can have thirty years of experience once, or one year of experience thirty times. And that experience can be beneficial, or damaging, or somewhere in between.

This book is concerned with here-and-now, experience-oriented environments for one major reason: because many people do learn things from these environments which have great impact for them as individuals. This stems from the fact that the goals of individual learning in groups are different from the goals of learning typical in school or college. In the latter case, learning is usually associated with something outside the individual – cognitive material or a technical skill. In Lewin's terms, formal education deals with the 'accomplishment' of something that is usually amenable to measurement. In group learning situations, by contrast, the goals of learning tend to be located within the individual: developing new insights about oneself as a person, analysing behaviour and its effect on others, understanding better the character of the relationships established with others, understanding better the impact one has on groups and organizations, and so forth. A theory of experiential group learning would be primarily a theory of personal change. Unlike most formal education settings, the processes by which a person learns experientially require taking into account the interaction between that individual and the group.

Characteristics of groups

Though group learning environments vary widely in their particular learning focus, a number of common characteristics that enhance (or are held to enhance) the potential for individual learning can be listed and discussed:

* a here-and-now concern in the group;
* the legitimization of *feelings* or emotions as appropriate and valuable material for analysis;
* a climate where people are free to *disclose* their feelings and perceptions, and to *feed back* reactions;
* a climate that makes provision for individual *choice* concerning change.

Each of these components will be discussed briefly.

The here-and-now focus

Perhaps the prime characteristic of learning in groups is concern with the here-and-now. In other learning environments, the development of understanding or new skills takes the form of analysing and assimilating information that comes from the outside, from what somebody else has said or done. In the experiential group, most learning stems directly from what is occurring at the time, or from what has occurred in the group's own idiosyncratic history.

The rationale underlying the here-and-now focus is an elementary best-evidence rule. The data that most help a person learn about self and others are those which are most readily and publicly available. Hence the emphasis on behaviour and reactions in the current group setting, rather than on data from some previous time or place outside the group. Note that here-and-now is a focus or an emphasis, not an invariable rule, depending on a particular trainer's orientation. In some groups, there-and-then autobiographical data are strictly out of bounds. In other groups, this information becomes admissible in so far as it is related to the present.

This concern with the here-and-now frequently brings the charge that because experiential learning groups tend not to use previously developed knowledge, they have an anti-intellectual bias. Undoubtedly, some trainers do devalue cognitive processes, research, and so forth. By and large, though, the here-and-now learning tasks with which participants in groups grapple have an exquisite and urgent intellectual base, if being intellectual is defined as thinking through intricate problems of human behaviour.

Feelings as appropriate and valuable material for analysis

Personal growth and the development of productive interpersonal relations are hampered by the constraints that our culture places on an individual when it comes to dealing openly with feelings. This applies to feelings of warmth and intimacy, as well as hostility. For example, one simply does not often tell one's teacher or boss that they are behaving in ways that make one feel of little worth and, therefore, angry. Such feelings usually are bottled up, and escape only in a big blow-up, if ever.

The cost/benefit analysis seems clear enough. People devalue their emotions and consider them to be inappropriate in problem-solving or work situations, for fear of alienating a friend, or of losing a promotion, perhaps even a job. In the process, however, they become emotionally malnutritioned and lose a bit of their humanity. Some people become so effective at suppressing their emotions, in fact, that they become unaware of which emotions they are experiencing, and when.

Learning groups depart radically from this sketch of the workaday world in encouraging the overt expression of feeling relative to the here-and-now. Winn (1969, p. 157) puts it this way: 'To acquire some insight, to obtain new awareness of himself, the participant must accept the raw data which the here-and-now generates. This acceptance implies willingness to express and deal with feelings as legitimate data for exploration.' Deeply-ingrained attitudes about learning may have to be changed. Basically, the learning process must place a substantial value on the emotional as well as the intellectual or rational.

Self-disclosure and feedback

Perhaps the most widespread reaction of participants in group learning situations is: 'I got a lot of new insights into myself.' Indeed, a focal thread that runs through most groups is the development of enhanced self-awareness so that a person may use self more productively. The primary vehicles for this type of learning are the complementary processes of self-disclosure and feedback.

The importance of self-disclosure may need some establishing for those accustomed to playing their life-cards close to their chests. Jourard (1971, p. 6) urges this powerful relationship between self-awareness and self-disclosure: '. . . no man can come to know himself except as an outcome of disclosing himself to another person.' As a person discloses his feelings and thoughts about himself to others so it becomes possible for others to feed back their perceptions of the disclosure, as well as their reactions to it.

Thus the act of self-disclosure initiates a process of both reality-testing and heightened intimacy. It is reality-testing in the sense that as an individual talks about himself, other group members can feed back their confirmation or denial of these self-perceptions. A relatively non-assertive man may believe he is undervalued by others. As he discloses this to the group, he may learn that quite the opposite is the case – that his style lends a certain stability to human relationships and is consequently highly valued, by at least some people. Or his own worst fears may be confirmed, from which comes the bitter-sweet but crucial conclusion that he is much the same person in his own eyes as in the eyes of others. To wit: he has the competence to see what is, which is the first central element in modifying what he dislikes in himself.

The potential for developing heightened intimacy through self-disclosure rests on the notion that when one person opens himself to the group, this constitutes an invitation for others to do likewise. It is a slow process, and not an easy one: as an individual talks about himself he becomes more vulnerable. The more open he is, the easier it becomes for others to take advantage of him, should they choose. Hence the importance of a climate of trust where people can be progressively more sure that their self-disclosure will not be taken advantage of by others as a vehicle for combat.

Two further points need to be made about self-disclosure. First, self-disclosure is least productive when it is conceived as confessional, particularly for sins committed some time in the past outside the group context. This may temporarily heighten intimacy – since misery often loves company – but there is no basis for satisfactory reality-testing. The best that can be expected is some sort of catharsis, with sympathetic listening.

The second point has to do with the major distinction between more disclosure and 'total disclosure', 'getting it all up-front'. Every individual will, and no doubt must, maintain a certain level of defences in the face of group pressures to disclose (Harrison, 1962). One myth that exists about experiential groups is that in order to learn a person must discard all his defences or have them ripped away by the group – so as to be fully open. To be sure, it is probably true that most people maintain their defences at unnecessarily high levels. But it is also true that to strip all defences will incapacitate a person as far as learning or even living is concerned.

One's defences constitute a type of handhold on reality. They are important to all of us, putting our interpersonal world in some sort of perspective. The purpose in personal learning groups is not to throw them all away, but to test them progressively in order to see at what level holding on to a particular defence inhibits learning and to determine whether, if a defence were to be discarded, it could be immobilizing.

The relationship between disclosure and feedback is two-way, of course. Thus the manner in which feedback is given to a person in a group has a direct bearing on the quality and quantity of self-disclosure in which a person is willing to engage, and vice versa. Ideally, feedback gives an individual the opportunity to find out how his behaviour is seen by others so that, if he wishes, he may change it. Counterproductive feedback only serves the needs of the giver (seeking dominance, for example), and usually provokes retaliation from the receiver. Generally speaking, productive feedback can be described as follows:

* Feedback is likely to be understood and accepted in more or less inverse proportion to the time elapsing between the situation inducing a reaction and the sharing of that reaction.

The longer the time, the less understanding and acceptance.
* Feedback is most likely to be understood and accepted when it describes specifics, such as particular patterns of behaviour or attitudes.
* Useful feedback reveals one's emotional reaction to another's behaviour without making moral or ethical judgements about the behaviour.
* Feedback is more meaningful when it comes from several people, not just one. Hence the significant difference between learning in a group, and learning with one or several other individuals in different places at different times (Mead, 1973).

Not only do such guidelines work, but they are clearly common sense. The sooner an individual knows how others react to his behaviour, the easier it is to recall what was done and why. The more feedback focuses on specific behaviour rather than overall personality issues, the more a person can contemplate choice or change. Telling another that he is a grossly overbearing person is not as helpful as describing the specific item of behaviour that made the recipient feel dominated. Not making value judgements about behaviour but conveying its emotional impact leaves recipients free to make their own judgements and decisions. This is a central quality in human relationships, because most people at most times would rather do things themselves. And finally, if the feedback comes from more than one person, the individual can get a more adequate picture rather than having to depend on only one report, which may be biased.

Learning to give productive interpersonal feedback is not an easy task. It involves being in touch with oneself, as well as learning to communicate in a way that allows the other to accept what is being said. Feedback need not be acted upon by the other to be effective. Rather, feedback needs to be given in such a way that the other person can make it part of his own data-bank about himself, to be used at his discretion.

Individual choice about change

A central notion in group learning is individual choice relative to change. In most formal education an individual has little choice about what he must do and learn. He must perform the prescribed task at a level acceptable to someone else, or fail. In group learning there are no fixed requirements or examinations to take. The tasks which an individual undertakes are chosen by him, and the ultimate criteria for success or failure are private ones. For example, a woman may be given some feedback that suggests that greater openness with her feelings would permit and encourage others to become closer. It then becomes her decision as to how she chooses to act on this feedback. She may take the position that she is quite satisfied with her relationships. Or she may decide that some of her interpersonal relationships are not exactly what she desires and that it would be worthwhile trying something different. The choice is hers.

Choice must also remain personal in order for an individual to 'own' the learning and implement the required change – even though there are times in the life of any group when the pressures on an individual to change become quite strong. This is usually because one or two members have experienced some sort of 'emotional high' as a result, perhaps, of self-disclosure that they found very freeing. Their thoughts are likely to be: 'If it was good for me, it will be better for you.' But this is not necessarily the case. What is duck soup for one may strike terror in the heart of another. Experiential groups are often a place to learn how to live and let live.

Models of individual change

So far we have discussed characteristics of experiential learning groups to do with interaction between members. The emphasis shifts now to a concern with the individual, and to four notions about the processes that occur as individuals learn, change or choose. The discussion will focus, in turn, on: Lewin's unfreezing schema; ideas developed by Jenkins; Rogers' concept of individual change having its roots in psychotherapy; and Hampden-Turner who sees individual change in groups as a cyclic process of psychosocial development leading to a higher sense of personal freedom and integrity.

Lewin: change as successive phases

At its most basic and undifferentiated level, the process through which an individual learns or changes or chooses in groups can be described in classic Lewinian terms of unfreezing, movement or change, and refreezing (Lewin, 1951), thus:[1]

Unfreezing		*Change*	*Refreezing*
A	B	C	D
Tension and the need for change are experienced by the person.	Changes are proposed by the person or by group members.	The person tests the proposed changes, especially those implying new behaviours and attitudes.	Those new behaviours and attitudes that prove to be more productive are reinforced and internalized.

Most people enter a group with a behavioural style that has been established over a period of years, and is relatively stable. They become part of a social environment which often very quickly fails to confirm previously learned concepts of how leaders should behave and how groups should operate. The effect of this situation is that tension develops as a participant's behavioural style is found wanting in the group situation (A). People respond to this state of change in different ways. They may disclose themselves, feed back to each other (B), make choices and test out (C) different ways of coping with themselves and each other. Some of the new things they try gain approval and reinforcement and become part of their new behavioural repertoire as refreezing takes place (D). And the process repeats itself as long as the group continues to confront new problems.

What has just been described is, of course, much oversimplified. But it does provide a framework from which to examine more specific concepts of personal change in learning groups.

Jenkins: change as secure disequilibrium

The late David Jenkins (1964), a student of Lewin's, makes four assumptions about the process of learning in groups:

1. Adapted from Golembiewski (1972, p. 177).

* The individual must feel some sense of basic *security* in the group situation.
* The individual must also experience a sense of *disequilibrium*.
* The individual needs to see what is occurring as some sort of *challenge* to himself.
* The challenge is used by the individual to start a process of *discovery*.

What is required, initially, is a very delicate balance between individual security and disequilibrium. An analogy may help: a ship can use an anchor to prevent excessive movement. But the anchors can be tethered so short and be so firmly imbedded that no real movement is possible. On the other hand, any movement (disequilibrium) that occurs ought not to be so aimless and disruptive as to deprive the individual of the opportunity of dropping his anchors firmly from time to time. If the disequilibrium becomes too great, either by group action or person-to-person confrontation, the chances are that the individual will become immobilized.

If the security-disequilibrium condition is in tolerable balance for the person, some sort of challenge may be experienced. If so, the individual may want to test out some new ways of relating to the group, or to some of its members. In other words, the motivating force is a pull and not a push. The potential learner is pulled along by the challenge of self-discovery. He is not pushed or coerced by forces external to him.

This process of self-discovery, for Jenkins, is the heart of the matter. Hence he raises a caution for group members and professional trainers as well. 'A real danger . . . is when we bring a person up to a point of discovery and, just as he is about to make the discovery, we *tell* him what it is. We deny him the discovery experience' (Jenkins, 1964, p. 1). The essential point here is one of ownership of the substance of new learning, as well as the process by which the new learning occurs. It is particularly important because most adults have, through formal institutional education, had the skills of self-discovery trained out of them. When people are *told* what they have discovered, or told what they should have discovered, they may feel a sense of diminished success, or even failure or shame. Even though the discovery may be important, its impact is diluted because the individual has not been allowed to make his own interpretations of the experience, thus cannot 'own' them.

Rogers: change as a new experiencing of self

A change model developed by Rogers (1961) as a way of understanding client change in psychotherapy also illuminates individual learning in groups. The model is process-oriented, and focuses on helping a person become more aware of his here-and-now feelings, and thus more able to interpret them in the light of current events rather than the past. The 'new feeling experience' is closely tied in to Rogers' non-directive style. Rogers' model involves seven stages:

* No problems are recognized or perceived.
* A loosening and flowing of symbolic expression occurs when the person feels accepted as he is.
* Further loosening develops as contradictions in experiencing are met.
* A gradual loosening of previously held constructs develops as the individual feels more understood and welcomed.
* Feelings are owned and expressed freely.
* The self as an object tends to disappear as the person experiences old feelings in the here-and-now context.
* New feelings are experienced in their immediacy, with relevance not only to the therapeutic situation but outside it as well.

The process that Rogers describes, then, begins with a state of little experiencing of self, or of experiencing self as an object. The goal is a condition in which a person is free to be and feel himself as he is. The process is *natural*, as long as the therapist behaves in a way that communicates acceptance, understanding, and welcoming of the individual as presented. In other words, Rogers maintains that, given the appropriate psychological climate, individual growth will take place simply because people have a predisposition to grow.

Many professionals in the group movement take issue with

the implications of this model – the purely accepting and understanding point of view. Others disagree with the idea that people are predisposed to grow, their own experience being different. Most people agree, however, that personal learning develops best when an individual is allowed to make his own judgements about his learning.

Hampden-Turner: investing and risking as central to change

Hampden-Turner (1966, 1970) has developed a revealing cyclical model of learning and psychosocial development (Figure 1). Its essential elements are:

* Each learner's competence is a mix of the quality of his cognition, clarity of identity, and degree of self-esteem.
* The learner invests this competence in the environment. From time to time investments involve risk beyond the person's competence.
* The risk is an effort to build a new bridge between self and another person, this bridge being built to the degree that the risky behaviour receives positive feedback. If the risk is negatively evaluated by the other person, a situation of conflict will develop.
* Whatever the nature of the feedback, the learner will modify his cognition, identity, and self-esteem (thus learning) and the process will come full cycle to begin again.

The cycle may spiral upward in a way that expands learning, or downward in a regressive reaction. In the former case, the altering of the person's existential state as a result of successful investments will increase motivation to invest and risk. As Hampden-Turner concludes, '. . . a series of successful investments (and the fearless comprehension of some unsuccessful investments) will cause *every segment of the cycle to enhance itself.* Cognition . . . will become even more powerful, more competence . . . will be experienced, greater self-confirmation . . . achieved . . . and so on' (Hampden-Turner, 1966, p. 368).

Examples of this cycle even though only parts of it take the form of observable behaviour, are common in group learning situations. They seem to be most vivid and common when a

Figure 1 A cyclic model of learning in groups (from Hampden-Turner, 1966, p. 368)

According to

(a) the quality of his cognition
(b) the clarity of his identity
(c) the extent of his self-esteem –

(j) The investor will attempt to integrate the feedback from this exchange into a mental map whose breadth and complexity are a measure of investing success.

(d) all three of which he orders into a purposeful synthesis of his experienced and anticipated competence –

(i) According to the enhancement (or reduction) experienced by the Other, the latter will reinvest (or avoid) in a manner which moves towards synergy (or conflict).

(e) the subject invests with a degree of autonomy in his human environment

(f) by periodically 'letting go' and risking a portion of his experienced competence.

(h) and seek self-confirmation through the impact of his invested competence upon the Other.

(g) He will thus try to 'bridge the distance' between himself and the Other

group moves towards sharing intimacy and warmth. Take the case of Jim. He saw himself as a warm person, yet he kept his warmth bottled up for fear of rejection should he share it physically with another. After much talk one day, he said: 'By gosh I'm going to do it.' He walked across the room and hugged a woman with whom he had scarcely interacted previously, but for whom he felt a certain closeness. His behaviour was well received, and seemed to have the observable effect of helping clarify his identity and enhancing his self-esteem. A burden was off his shoulders; he saw his sense of competence as a person confirmed and became more able to invest himself in the group.

Jim's behaviour had effects on other group members. By his own action he legitimated and encouraged investment and risk on the part of other members of the group. In effect, he changed the norms of the group, enabling others to engage in behaviour through which they could satisfy some of their own learning needs.

There are other implications in Hampden-Turner's model. A brief discussion of two will illustrate the range of possibilities. Firstly, it seems reasonable to suppose that the processes involved in the model clarify Jenkins' concern with discovery. What Hampden-Turner has done, to our way of thinking, is to break down the different steps in personal discovery and thus direct attention to specific parts of the process when learning is blocked.

Secondly, given that experience does not of itself imply learning, Hampden-Turner has described some major personal and interpersonal conditions under which experiential learning takes place. The theoretical and practical potentials of the model, then, go far beyond the problems of learning in groups.

The aim of this chapter has been to provide the reader with some frames of reference with which to describe the processes by which people learn in groups. Two other goals have been to dispel any notions of mysticism that may surround group learning, and to discourage the idea that something good will happen 'if we only had a group'.

3   Laboratory Education

The previous chapters have dealt with learning groups as if they were all cast in the same mould. In fact there is a wide variety of experiential groups, which all come under the general heading of 'laboratory education'. The aim of this chapter is to clarify the concept. It will close with the question of whether or not what happens in experiential groups is primarily a matter of educational training or of therapy.

Four aspects of laboratory education
Laboratory education as experimentation

Most of the readers of this book have taken a laboratory science course in school or college in which they were required to perform certain experiments, to understand scientific concepts better. The essential elements of experimentation are to try something, and then observe what happens. Laboratory education involves the application of scientific methods of experimentation and observation to individual and group behaviour. A major difference, of course, is that the individual is experimenting with himself, rather than something outside himself. Many group learning settings are called laboratories so as to convey the idea that participants will be encouraged to experiment beyond their usual patterns of interacting with individuals and groups.

The critical learning issue in laboratory education is not the absorption and regurgitation of externally predetermined content, as in most classrooms. Laboratory education puts the onus for learning on the individual to create through his own behaviour and skills human situations from which he can learn.

Laboratory education as analogous to society

These comments do not imply that laboratories are structureless, or that no skilled professional personnel are present as 'teachers'. In a way, laboratory education involves a great deal of structure; and a 'teacher' is usually present. The difference is that the structure is much more open-ended than in most learning situations, especially as to the issues around which learning may take place. Moreover, the teacher (trainer) role in laboratory education differs markedly from that of a leader in a typical teaching–learning situation. Instead of emphasizing his role as a conveyer of knowledge, the laboratory educator's role is to enable group members to become their own analysers, experimenters, and synthesizers.

Laboratory education basically involves miniature societies for learning, societies which place on a small stage problems like those which members face in life. Hence the basic challenge of laboratory education is the creation '. . . for the purposes of analysis and practice, [of] group situations . . . where the same basic factors of individual and group relations are present as in the pressing problem situation of each person back home' (Bradford, 1953, p. 14). Thus, laboratory education seeks to present the learner with an analogue of the interpersonal, group, or organizational systems he confronts in daily life, with the crucial difference, of course, that in a laboratory the learner is not playing for keeps.

Laboratory education as process-oriented

Perhaps *the* distinguishing feature of the laboratory learning model is its concern with the primacy of *process* issues – at personal, interpersonal, group, or organizational levels – as contrasted with issues of *content*. Issues of content refer to the substance of communications. In contrast, issues of process are concerned with:

* what any specific content means in the context of some particular stage of development of some group;
* how the group members behave and deal with each other.

Process and content are not easily separated. Indeed, learning how to disentangle and differentiate the two is one of the essential tasks of laboratory education. For example, members of a group may engage in an animated discussion about dominating leadership. On the process level, the discussion may really refer to members' reactions to their own group experience. Some finely-tuned observational and analytical skills are required to capture the real emphasis. And that emphasis is critical.

Some greater sense of the complexity of process analysis can be economically suggested. In terms of behaviour, process orientation has to do with such things as who does most of the talking, patterns of communications and influence, how group decisions are made, the rituals of gaining and maintaining psychological membership in the group, and so forth.

Though some repetition of points made earlier is involved, another and more detailed way to convey the scope of the process orientation underlying laboratory education is to list the conditions for laboratory learning (National Training Laboratories Institute, n.d.) necessary for participants to reach training goals. These are:

* *Presentation of self:* until the individual has an opportunity to reveal the way he sees things and does things, little basis for improvement and change exists.
* *Feedback:* individuals do not on their own learn very well from their experiences. They learn better from bringing out the essential patterns of purposes, motives, and behaviour in a situation where others give them clear and accurate information about the relevancy and effectiveness of their behaviour.
* *Atmosphere:* an atmosphere of trust and non-defensiveness is necessary for people, to be willing to expose their behaviour and purposes, as well as to accept feedback.
* *Cognitive map:* knowledge from research, theory, and experience is important in helping the individual understand experiences and generalize from them. Normally, information is most effective when it follows experience and feedback.
* *Experimentation:* unless there is opportunity to try out new

patterns of thought and behaviour, they are unlikely to become a part of the individual's repertoire. Without experimental efforts relevant change is difficult to make.

* *Practice:* equally important is the need to practise new approaches so that the individual can gain security in assessing expanded or novel patterns of behaviours or attitudes.
* *Application:* unless learning and change can be applied to home situations, they are not likely to be effective or lasting. Attention needs to be given to helping individuals plan applications at home.
* *Relearning how to learn:* because much of our academic experience has led us to believe that we learn from listening to authorities, individuals frequently need to learn how to learn from presentation-feedback-experimentation.

These conditions suggest that laboratory education involves a learning environment in which the focus is not on subject matter *per se*, but on the self as an interacting and perceiving organism. This does not deny the importance of cognition; it merely puts it in perspective, showing that in matters of behavioural change cognition is the ground and not the figure. An atmosphere of trust is essential so that individuals are free to give and receive feedback about their behaviour, and can experiment with and practise new forms of behaviour.

Laboratory education: its meta-goals

Transcending the goals and processes outlined above, several meta-goals provide the philosophical rationale for the type of learning with which we are concerned. These meta-goals (Bennis, 1962) were not arrived at in a deductive fashion. No one sat down prior to the development of laboratory education and said, 'These goals will guide what we do in a lab.' Rather, these meta-goals developed out of a sense of experience which seemed to repeat itself, and they are described as:

* expanded consciousness and recognition of choice;
* a spirit of inquiry;
* authenticity in interpersonal relations;
* a collaborative conception of the authority relationship.

These meta-goals can be described briefly. To begin with, most of us live and work in situations where our perceptions and our estimates of what is and what can be are limited, and sometimes severely so. The underlying constraints are diverse. They include organizational goals, communications patterns, the decision-making structure, personnel policies, norms pertaining to authority relations or levels of interpersonal intimacy, and so forth. The effect of such constraints is to create a sort of 'tunnel vision'. That is, the constraints limit what we see and the range of choices we consider when making decisions about ourselves, our relations with other people, or elements of organizational life. Formal or informal mechanisms often defeat the purpose for which they were designed, namely, to help an individual or an organization achieve self-awareness so that appropriate choices can be made. In a laboratory structure and processes put a premium on the individual's awareness of the existential phenomena of the moment, and attempt to activate a wider range of choices than might ordinarily be the case. The specific dynamics of encouraging recognition of a wider range of choices are complicated and fluid. They will be discussed more fully in chapter 4, which deals with specific T-group dynamics.

According to Bennis, the meta-goal concerned with expanding choices bears a close relationship to that of 'a spirit of inquiry' (Bennis, 1962, p. 2). The central question raised over and over again in group experiences is: What is happening and why? The 'why' is crucial. For it suggests that investigation of the human condition is relevant and necessary; that the behaviour of individuals, groups, and organizations is a legitimate subject for inquiry outside the psychological laboratory or the therapist's office; and that the very act of inquiring can be freeing in itself. The development of a spirit of inquiry contrasts sharply with the overt and covert norms in the day-to-day life of most people. One advances in life, so we have been taught, not by raising questions about the norms of an organization or of society but by accepting them: 'My country, right or wrong.' Those who disagree and turn their questions into action are thought non-patriotic or criminal and lacking a sense of moral duty.

An emphasis on authenticity in interpersonal relationships pervades all laboratory settings. 'Authentic relationships are ... those relationships in which an individual enhances his sense of self and other awareness and acceptance in such a way that others can do the same' (Argyris, 1962, p. 21). Development of the skill of establishing authentic relationships with another is difficult. It involves learning to be in touch with what one is experiencing, both on the cognitive and feeling level, and being able to communicate it to another in a manner which encourages reciprocation. Authenticity is like tennis: the game cannot be played by a person in isolation. Hence, in laboratories *the* question is: 'How are you feeling?' Once more, this third meta-goal of laboratory education contrasts with the expectations of everyday life. Often common wisdom and authenticity are at odds, as in the advice that one must keep one's feelings to oneself in order not to disrupt the organization. There certainly *are* situations in which it is inappropriate to express one's feelings at the moment. But doing so implies a cost, and is often overdone, so that it can be a disservice to both the individual and organization that are ostensibly protected.

The fourth meta-goal of laboratory education, a collaborative concept of the authority relationship, departs most radically from common wisdom. If authority relationships are on a continuum with one pole representing power and coercive control, and the other collegiality and mutual influence, laboratory relationships would be set towards the collegial end of the scale; bureaucratic authority relationships would be at the other end.

This position is consistent with the theme that has run throughout this discussion of meta-goals: namely, that as well as being concerned with developing a higher level of personal and interpersonal behavioural and diagnostic skill, laboratory education is also concerned with a more humanistic approach to how people can relate to each other in the world of work. The collaborative concept of authority suggests that, regardless of authority relationships, it is possible for people to collaborate in setting work goals, in producing, and evaluating production. In the process of such work each person has the

Figure 2 Basic laboratories in human interaction (from Lubin and Eddy, 1970, p. 314)

Design focus	Individual and organizational relevance	Experiences
Personal and interpersonal	more openness and honesty in dealing with self and others/reduced defensiveness and game-type behaviour/increased ability to learn from one's own behaviour/expanded awareness to growth potential/increased awareness of racially conditioned feelings and attitudes	T-groups Nonverbal Painting Improvisation and fantasy Body movement Interpersonal confrontation Racial confrontation
	improved communication with others/development of new ways of working with others/locating feelings that block satisfactory and effective relationships, and bringing these out for examination/ working for creative resolution to conflict	
Intergroup	effects on your behaviour when your group is working with another group/looking at your loyalties in multigroup operations/diagnosing intragroup problems brought on by intergroup work/examining the effect of different racial mixtures	T-groups Competitive and collaborative exercises Observation of groups Conflict models Multiple loyalty simulations Construction of conceptual models
	examining intergroup consultation, cooperation, and competition (corresponds to interdepartmental relationships in a firm)/how changes can be made between groups/looking at payoffs for collaboration and competition/conceptualizing and confronting conflict, including that generated by racial differences	

Design focus	Individual and organizational relevance	Experiences
	increasing ability to act in different ways in a group and to live with different types of group climate, including that in which race is a problem/getting feedback on your group style and work methods/using your own feelings to help understand group process/feeling freer in groups	T-groups Role analysis Cluster and large groups Team building Consultation
Group	understanding stages of group life and development/leadership and membership in groups (such as departments, task forces, teams, classes)/learning why some problems get 'solved' over and over, and why some decisions don't stick/constructive methods for dealing with problem members/experimenting with different methods for handling racially generated problems	Helping relationships Construction of conceptual models Group problem-solving exercises

Figures 3 The primary focus of different types of laboratories (from Buchanan and Reisel, 1972, p. 2)

	Type of Laboratory					
Focus	Personal Growth HR	Group Basic HR	Inter-Group HR	Organizational*	Vocational†
Self-Self	Primary	Secondary	Tertiary	Tertiary	Secondary
Self-Other	Primary	Secondary	Secondary	Secondary	Primary
Self-Group	Secondary	Primary	Secondary	Secondary	Primary
Self-Organization	Tertiary	Secondary	Primary	Primary	Primary
Self-Vocation	Tertiary	Tertiary	Tertiary	Primary	Primary

*This category includes laboratories conducted for specific organizations, such as a corporation or a school district.

†This category includes laboratories for such groups as educators, or business managers who are not from the same company.

opportunity to use his resources and those of the other in reciprocal fashion.

In summary, then, laboratory education is directed towards change and choice, and therefore towards how they are induced in human, group, and organizational relationships. Our position is that more productive ways of helping people relate to each other, to groups, and organizations can be discovered; that little is known even though the notions discussed above show that a good start has been made; and that the quest for these more creative relationships is of primary importance to our present and our future.

Types of laboratories

The scope of laboratory education is extremely wide and it is crucial to make some broad differentiations between group experiences. In so doing, we follow Lubin and Eddy (1970, p. 314), who differentiate laboratories according to their design focus, as personal or interpersonal, intergroup, or group. Figure 2 illustrates the particular kinds of learning anticipated from each of the three designs. The table also illustrates the variety of experiences that may be utilized within each type of learning design to further its own specific goals. Note that T-groups are included regardless of the focus of the laboratory.

Buchanan and Reisel (1972) also use the 'focus' notion. As Figure 3 indicates, each focus places emphasis on the self. That is, various kinds of laboratories can be concerned with learning about the self in relationship to five other systems, including the self as system and extending to vocational systems:

* A self–self laboratory is concerned primarily with personal growth. The data base for learning is intrapersonal.
* A self–other laboratory focuses on interpersonal relationships. Participants are encouraged to seek out data concerning, for example, the impact of their behaviour on others and the manner in which they deal with others.
* In a self–group laboratory learning concerns the person and the manner in which he relates to a group as a social entity. Questions of influence styles and the quality of group membership become important.

* Self–organization laboratories give primary attention to the individual as a member of a large organization. Laboratories of this type frequently involve experiences in conditions of intergroup competition, conflict, and cooperation.
* Self–vocation laboratories are oriented towards the person as a worker; the feelings, aspirations, and life-meaning that he derives from his occupation.

The Buchanan-Reisel typology indicates the primacy of different combinations of activities in each laboratory type. For example, a self–organization focus will be prominent in laboratories that are concerned with intergroup relationships, organizational relationships, or vocational problems. Similarly, the self–self focus is central in personal-growth learning situations, but gets only secondary or tertiary attention in the other laboratory types.

Some variants of group learning

The focal concern in this book is the classical T-group setting, but it is a mistake to think that 'T-group' is a unitary concept. The following pages consider a number of important variants of T-groups including the most bizarre aberration of experiential learning that we know of.

Study groups

Klein and Astrachan (1971) contrasted the theoretical orientation of T-groups and what they call study groups. The goals of each are similar – to learn about group and individual behaviour in the here-and-now – but their starting points are different. These differences have a cultural genesis.

The T-group is an American product, and its basic assumptions tend to reflect central concerns in American life. Hence, the T-group emphasizes the equality and interdependence of its members as the primary and most productive way they can learn to become more self-aware, skilled, and cognizant of the dynamics of group life. This orientation is seen in the T-group trainer's role as he '. . . acts an examplar of "good member" behavior, implementing the goals of the group (such as that of lowering defenses); he gives "straight" but non-judgmental feedback, and he is "open" in the recognition and acceptance of his own feelings' (Klein and Astrachan, 1971, p. 666). Although individual trainers bring their own group development theories to bear, the major frame of reference is Lewinian social psychology with its emphasis on the interdependent sharing of resources.

The concept of the study group is British in origin, and reflects different structuring assumptions. For example, rather than assuming equality of group members, study groups primarily deal with authority issues. Questions of individual relationships to authority figures seem to be more pervasive in Britain than are issues of interdependence.

The differences in structuring assumptions between T-groups and study groups generate a host of contrasts. For example, the study group approaches the dynamics of group life from a Freudian position. This reflects the fact that the study group concept was developed at the Tavistock Clinic and Institute of Human Relations where the dominant clinical theory is a Freudian one; also that theory's elitist and conservative biases contrast sharply with the more optimistic and eclectic theory-base underlying most T-groups. Moreover, the study group places little emphasis on the dynamics of individual behaviour, reserving its main study for group dynamics. The convenor of the study is called 'consultant', and this is perhaps the key point. His role is to reflect the group's orientation: '... he is an observer of, and commentator on, group actions and reactions. He remains "detached", and his nondirective and remote behavior is designed to frustrate members' dependency needs; this frustration in turn increases their anxiety and produces anger toward him' (Klein and Astrachan, 1971, p. 664). The deeper level goals of this deliberate production of anxiety are to create both feelings and fantasies about authority – in this case, the consultant – which become the central here-and-now data to be analysed.

It is easier to write about the 'pure form' of the study group than of the T-group. The style and goals of T-group trainers are much more apt to vary than those of study group consultants. Trainers tend to represent a wide variety of academic backgrounds, if nothing else, while the Tavistock consultants much more frequently come from a similar training and theoretical mould.

Two additional points are worth noting in this discussion of T-groups and study groups. First, though Klein and Astrachan draw sharp contrasts between the two, in practice, as far as group development is concerned, participants indicate that the differences get blurred. For example, people who have been in both types of groups report similar personal learnings. They are quite likely to recall, however, the cool detachment of the study group consultant in contrast to the more involved T-group trainer. Second, it would be a mistake to infer that study groups are confined to England and T-groups to the United States. T-groups are more widespread in both countries. But it seems likely that each is having an impact on the other.

Encounter groups

We have often been asked whether T-groups are the same thing as encounter groups. And just as commonly, we hedge. For the literature is not very helpful in spelling out any systematic differences. And experience is even more disorderly.

So we approach the comparison of T-groups and encounter groups gently. The term 'encounter' was apparently coined by Rogers. Solomon and Berzon (1972, p. xii) recall their experiences at the Western Behavioral Sciences Institute in California: 'In the early 1960s, they were most often called sensitivity training groups. Several years later, Carl Rogers . . . gave these groups the name Basic Encounter. The *basic* did not stick. The *encounter* did.'

Encounter group is certainly a catchier term than T-group. Are we then just dealing with different terminology? Egan (1970, Preface) apparently thought so when he prefaced his book *Encounter* with these comments: 'This book is about a small group experience that has many names – basic encounter group, a laboratory in interpersonal relations, sensitivity training, a basic human relations laboratory, or an inter-personal-growth-oriented T-group.' Burton (1969, p. 2), while not contrasting encounter groups with other kinds of groups, describes them in terms that do seem to make a difference. 'Encounter groups are "soul" groups . . . There is no agenda. What purpose there is is merely to live more fully and experience more deeply. Personal history and conflict are set aside so that living itself may be experienced. In encounter living, it is thus hoped, some of the answers to existence may be found.'

While there are no definite boundary lines, and many observers lump T-groups and encounter groups together, there are many significant differences. Consider Burton's description of encounter groups as 'soul' groups with a fundamental goal of finding some answers to existence. This orientation is clearly not the one that Klein and Astrachan had in mind as they discussed study groups. Nor is it our framework as we work in T-group settings. This is not to disparage Burton's point of view, but simply to note that there can be major differences between a traditional T-group and *some* encounter groups.

The sense of 'encounter' as referring to complex learning technologies that can differ significantly from one another is well established by the approach taken in the Lieberman, Yalom and Miles (1973) research. To include all major theoretical approaches to group learning they selected professional leaders who represented ten widely used technologies, including the traditional T-group approach. The remaining nine were described by Lieberman, Yalom and Miles (1973, pp. 11–13) as:

* *Gestalt Therapy.* Gestalt therapy has been a militant, proselytizing movement with major centres in New York, California, and Cleveland. Gestalt stresses the wholeness of the individual. Change is viewed as a subintellectual process which is mediated by helping the individual get in touch with the primitive wisdom of the body. When the late Fritz Perls, founder of the Gestalt school, operated Gestalt groups, there was little use of the group, or, for that matter, the other group members. There was an empty chair, 'the hot seat', next to the leader to which the members came one by one to 'work' with the leader. In Gestalt-oriented en-

counter, much emphasis is placed on heightened emotionality, on understanding what the body is telling one by its posture, by its numerous autonomic and muscular-skeletal messages. The leader often helps members to resolve inner conflict by holding dialogues between the disparate parts of the psyche. The participation of the other members is minimal; often their primary function is simply to verify by their presence, like the all-seeing Greek chorus.

* *Transactional Analytic.* Eric Berne (1961) first introduced the term 'transactional analysis' and a distinct style of small group leadership based on this method. Not unlike the Gestalt groups, the 'work' is done by the leader with each of the group members in turn. Berne often spoke of therapy *in* a group rather than *with* a group. The term transactional analysis refers to the transactions between ego states (parent, child, and adult) *within* one individual rather than transactions among individuals.

* *Esalen Eclectic.* William Schutz in his book *Joy* (1967) describes a basic approach to the encounter group and a number of techniques for accelerating the developmental pace of the group. These include an emphasis both on the experiencing and deepening of interpersonal relationships and on the liberating of somatic restrictions. By breaking free from social and muscular inhibitions, people learn to experience their own bodies and other people in a different and fuller sense. The group leader's focus is on both the individual and the interpersonal relationships within the group. Often structural interventions may be suggested by the leader to help members shuck constricting inhibitions. The emphasis is on doing and experiencing; the cause, the meaning of the persisting restrictions is of minor consequence.

* *Personal Growth (National Training Laboratory Groups, Western Style).* Personal growth leaders are grounded in the NTL sensitivity group approach, but have shifted their emphasis from the group to a Rogerian conception of the individual. Most of the leader's attention is centred on interpersonal or intrapersonal dynamics; rarely does he focus on 'the group'. He has a liberating model of personal develop-

ment and does not object to the concept of group therapy for normals. Most leaders of this school see little distinction between personal growth and psychotherapy.

* *Synanon.* The Synanon group (referred to as the Synanon game) is grossly different from any of the other types. It emphasizes the expression of anger; the game is 'put' on each member in turn, and the other members systematically explore and attack him presumably in the belief that if one is attacked in his weakest areas long enough he will grow stronger in them. It is termed a game perhaps because once the group is over the atmosphere changes quickly to one of warm support.

* *Psychodrama.* To consider psychodrama as a type of encounter group is to introduce slippage in logic, since psychodrama or role-playing is used as an aid, or an auxiliary technique, in many encounter formats. Some encounter group leaders, however, structure their groups predominantly as psychodrama or role-playing experiences. (The Moreno purist may shudder at this vulgarization, since these groups are obviously not employing psychodrama in its classic sense.)

* *Marathon.* The marathon or time-extended group meeting, first introduced by George Bach, has become a household concept in the crazy quilt world of the encounter group. A marathon group meets for long stretches of time: twelve, twenty-four, or, occasionally, an heroic forty-eight hours without pause. Members may take short sleep periods but generally the group is continuous. Intensive psychological contact together with sheer physical exhaustion serve to accelerate the movement and the pace of interaction. 'Marathon-oriented' encounter leaders claim that the power generated by this hyperbolical togetherness can in a single week-end induce more personal change than months, even years, of spaced, 'diluted' meetings. The marathon format implies more than sheer form. Affixed to the form are certain core substantive principles: high intensity, involvement, interpersonal honesty, and confrontation. Defence mechanisms are not tolerated; the members must quickly

jettison them or the group strips or vigorously sands them away.

* *Psychoanalytically Oriented.* The term 'psychoanalytic encounter group' would have persuaded Fenichel that the American Philistines had overrun the last bastion of the classical psychoanalytic edifice. This category is intended to represent encounter groups led by conservative, analytically oriented clinicians. These groups are generally, but not always, led for students in the helping professions; they focus on the dynamics and the individual in the group, especially from the perspective of his personal historical development. They tend to be less emotionally charged, more rationally based with heavier focus on intellectual mastery of group dynamics as well as inter- and intrapersonal forces operating in the group.

* *Encounter Tapes* (*Leaderless Groups*). Many encounter groups are self-directed; they have no officially designated leader, though often an unofficial leader emerges from the ranks of the members. Elizabeth Berzon investigated several methods of increasing the efficacy of leaderless groups, attempting to understand the precise contributions of the leader and to build these functions into the group through some artificial means. She has developed a highly sophisticated set of tape recordings which members play during each meeting of an encounter group. These tapes are marketed under the trade name of 'encountertapes' by Bell and Howell, and have gained widespread use. The tape programme uses a variety of structured exercises (prescribed sets of interaction among members as a total group, among pairs, and occasionally as individuals in meditation) to construct a cohesive, 'warm', and unthreatening group climate. Members are taught through doing as well as through explanations to emphasize relationships, feedback, and reflection.

These approaches to laboratory education are not mutually exclusive, although they can differ fundamentally in process and content. For example, the Gestalt therapy model differs in significant particulars from the T-group with which this book essentially deals. Problems considered might be similar, but they would be analysed in different ways. A transactional analysis group, similarly, would be likely to take a different approach to the diagnosis of interpersonal conflict than would a Synanon group. In addition, the role of the leader varies from a very central place in a Gestalt group to one of 'no leader' in the encounter tape situation.

But labels can sometimes be misleading as well as instructive. Thus Lieberman, Yalom and Miles (1973) argue that the style and applied theory of the professional resource person who oversees or directs the group is apparently more important than the kind of experience that is advertised. Consequently, if people take part in several different group experiences, as many do, they often experience some overlap in both the substance and process of what occurred. Similarly, many people might report diverse experiences even in 'similar' groups, given different trainer styles. The key element seems to be the theory or focus around which a professional resource person moulds a specific experience.

A wildly bizarre use of the learning group

The experiential group learning field has been subject to no legal or professional accreditation or certification procedures.[1] Anyone, then, can lead a group and in any manner he chooses, a situation that has led to the development of some strange group experiences. The most bizarre situation which we know about is related by Church and Carnes (1972).

The training session in question was sponsored by one local unit of a large organization. It was held in a motel in California and lasted four days. There were twenty-four male participants, most of whom were there because the company for which they worked, which had some sort of interest in the training agency, made it clear that if the men wished to advance in the company it would be a good idea to attend. The fee for each participant was one thousand dollars. If a man left before the four days

1. A new organization, the International Association of Applied Social Scientists, has been established. Its primary mission has been to accredit qualified laboratory educators, but its accreditation is a professional matter and has no legal base at present.

were up, he forfeited his fee. In addition, if a person did leave, his room-mate also would be required to leave and forfeit his fee, and perhaps run the risk of jeopardizing his position in the organization which had urged his attendance. At least, this is what the men were told. Each participant was also required to sign a statement which released the trainers from responsibility for any harm that might come as a result of the experience.

For most of the four days, the men lived in the group room, whose centre was called The Pit. They had very little sleep and ate military rations. Among other items, The Pit included a man-sized cage, a coffin, also man-sized, an eight foot by five foot wood cross, and a hangman's noose. The rules relative to physical contact were that (1) hitting in the face with a closed fist was forbidden to all except the instructors, (2) hitting the body with a closed fist was allowed and encouraged, and (3) no one was ever to hit an instructor. In addition, unquestioned obedience to the instructors was an absolute requirement.

The goal of the experience was to create leaders by bringing out the truth and honesty in each participant. In order to do this, the director said: 'We *will* . . . break through all the lies you live with and teach you to lead better, more truthful lives' (Church and Carnes, 1972, p. 7).

Most of the men submitted to demeaning and dehumanizing behaviour as they sought their moment of 'truth'. This included being put in the coffin or cage, tied to the cross, eating garbage and excrement, and being struck both by the instructors and their fellow group members. Participants were literally battered, physically and psychologically.

It is a chilling story, but fascinating from the point of view of trying to answer the question of why otherwise average people would both voluntarily submit to degradation and, at the same time, inflict it on others. Fear? Ambition? The quest for the 'truth'? Power? The answers are unclear, but they need to be sought.

Laboratory education or group therapy?

A question continually raised about laboratory learning groups is whether or not what goes on in them really is not group therapy in disguise. Further, the question goes, if it is therapy, are not those who engage in conducting 'training' guilty of practising medicine without a qualification or, at least, passing themselves off as healers?

Answers to these questions have an elusive quality, due to the difficulty of distinguishing education from therapy. The National Training Laboratories Institute (1969, p. 7) in its publication *Standards for the Use of the Laboratory Method* makes the statement: 'Insofar as it is possible to distinguish between education and psychotherapy, NTL Institute programmes are applied for educational, not psychotherapeutic, purposes. The Institute does not design or conduct programmes to cure or alleviate pathological mental or emotional conditions.' Sensitivity training, then, is considered as a learning technology which can help most people grow in both their understanding and their capacity to relate to individuals, groups, and organizations. It is not seen as a vehicle for overcoming serious personality defects or as a way of dealing with mental illness.

In practice, of course, the problem is not as clear-cut as the last paragraph suggests. Some still argue that sensitivity training is therapy under a different name, even given the most fastidious of intentions, for two major reasons.

Firstly, the nature of the learning that many people achieve in a group *does* possess a therapeutic quality.

Those who try to distinguish education and therapy would agree that group experiences can be helpful and promote growth, but in a way different from a psychotherapy group. For example, if gaining insight and understanding into oneself is equated with therapy, then certainly much of this takes place in sensitivity training. However, the kind of insight which tends to develop in a T-group is usually related to the situation of the moment and is not of the intrapsychic variety associated with therapy. Thus, if a person has fed back to him the reaction that his joking style makes some people not take him seriously at work, he has achieved an insight into the effects of his behaviour of which he may have been previously unaware. But it is at this point that sensitivity training departs from most individual therapy. That is, the aims of certain forms of therapy would then be served by engaging in an analysis of how he got that way. This process might be auto-biographical, with the assistance of symbolic interpretation on the part of the therapist. The idea would be that if the individual could understand the genesis of his behaviour he would be more of a whole person, potentially freer from any neurotic anxieties deriving from these genetic roots, and better able to alter his behaviour.

In the sensitivity training situation, the autobiographical tactic tends to be discouraged, as are references to unconscious motivation. The issue in the example above, in contrast, might be: what are the alternative ways available to the person for dealing with himself so that if he wanted to joke he could do so and not 'turn people off'. Or he might discover that others have found him to be using humour to protect himself from close relationships, or to cover up his hostility. Such a discovery might help him deal with himself better, whether that discovery is educational or therapeutic.

The boundary lines between the goals and strategies of therapy and group learning environments are not clean and neat. But they do suggest some significant points of difference.[1]

The second basic reason for the training–therapy problem is an accident of history. Those responsible for the early development of sensitivity training came primarily from the fields of social psychology and adult education. Their concerns focused on group dynamics and the development of behavioural skills, the potential self-insight and awareness of the training experience notwithstanding. However, as the group training approach achieved wider recognition, it attracted professional personnel whose background was in either clinical psychology or psychiatry. Quite naturally, these people had interests oriented towards the person more than the group. The groups they led tended to have more of a therapeutic flavour than an existential and behavioural one.

This influence of clinically-oriented specialists on sensitivity

1. For a more detailed discussion of the differences between T-groups and group therapy, see Yalom, (1970), especially.

training should not be taken as unfortunate or bad. Indeed, they have contributed much to our understanding of the dynamics of individual behaviour in group settings. And, patently, learning more about group phenomena and potential has influenced some therapists to alter their focus and style. The training–therapy issue remains, however. It is, perhaps, a burden that the laboratory method will have to bear for some time to come, while efforts are made to generate appropriate expectations in potential participants and to screen out those individuals in need of therapy.

This chapter has looked at the broad spectrum of laboratory education and the various group learning typologies that have developed around it. In the next chapter we become specific about the internal dynamics of the traditional T-group model as the prototype of experiential group learning environments.

4 Distinguishing Features of the T-group

The T-group, the heart of the sensitivity training laboratory, is so powerful that it absorbs the major portion of most participants' emotional energy during a lab. It is usually the most memorable and remembered part of their experience.

This chapter should furnish the reader with a clearer picture of why and how it is so memorable. However, though the reader may end up knowing about the T-group, he will not know it *personally*. *Knowing* a T-group means *experiencing* it.

The T-group as social microcosm

Of the many ways that might be chosen to conceptualize a T-group, the most useful is to view it as a developing society in microcosm. The T-group is an analogue of life, and consequently can help generate insight into problems of communication, leadership, problem-solving, norm development, conflict, etc, that most people confront in their day-to-day lives in families, at work, and so on. For example, every T-group generates a number of sub-groups which affect the group's development and manner of work. This is just like life 'out there'. What is different is that in the T-group, 'in here', the formulation, behaviour, and motivations of these sub-groups are open to examination and analysis.

Seeing the T-group as a miniature society has another advantage, which is academically oriented. Many trainers are directly interested in the production of knowledge as well as its application. The societal approach to understanding the T-group enables trainers to view the group's processes on the social system level of analysis, and hence can contribute to a comprehensive social theory. For example, cause/effect relationships are amenable to experimentation and analysis in a T-group.

This point is not trivial. Some people prefer to view the T-group as an aggregate in which people are only enabled to test their behaviour against the behaviour of others openly and directly. Such observers may accuse the proponents of the T-group-as-microcosm of diluting the emotional experience. The latter, in turn, can accuse their accusers of being anti-intellectual.

The idea that learning about complex social systems or large organizations can derive from a small group experience may strike the reader as a bit far-fetched. But closer examination indicates that the potential for such learning does, indeed, exist in every T-group. This position is based on the work of Weick (1969) who suggests that, for most purposes, a group of even only nine people contains the basic relationships of authority and control which are critical in all social systems, large or small. For example, complex coalitions can be formed in a group of nine; love and anger can be exchanged; inter-group competition and conflict, or isolation, or deviance, also can occur. 'If we can understand how nine people go about the work of getting organized, producing, dissolving, and re-structuring, then we shouldn't find many surprises when we watch 1,000 people go through the same activities' (Weick, 1969, p. 25).

How a T-group starts

Every trainer has his own way of starting a T-group, but certain themes become clear, even if the trainer is silent! Usually, for example, the trainer will say something like:

We'll be meeting together in this, our T-group, throughout the lab. The purpose of our group is to investigate what happens as we try to work together, to look at our own behaviour and our relationships with other members of the group. Our concerns will focus on the 'here-and-now' – what is going on in this group – and not the 'there-and-then' – what has transpired outside of this group or in our home situation. 'Ve will be behaviourally-oriented and not personality-oriented. Our T-group is a laboratory and by that I mean that it will probably be helpful if we can experiment with new ways of behaving and test them out against other people. Throughout our time together we will, in fact, be building a miniature society. If we wish to we can probably learn a lot about other social systems from analysing our own. Remember, the critical question for us will be, 'What is happening to us here and why is it happening?' The question that is not important is, 'Why are you that kind of a person?' What I will try and do is help us answer the questions that confront us.

At this point, the trainer often stops and withdraws from the kind of active participation which might be expected from a group leader. The ensuing silence may last anywhere from a few seconds to many minutes. If this silence endures for more than just a few moments it is likely to be accompanied by embarrassed giggles, outright laughter, or even mock screams of despair! Soon, however, some form of focused behaviour develops which may be directed at the trainer. e.g. 'Can you be more specific?' or 'Would you repeat what you said?' Or a member may suggest that the group establish a goal or get a topic, because the trainer clearly will not do it for them. Regardless of what is said or done, the group has started and its silence, giggles or laughter, or any verbal comments, provide material for analysis.

Essentially, what has happened is that the trainer has produced a power vacuum, by his rather vague introduction and subsequent withdrawal from active participation. The effect is to produce, for most people, discomfort because their expectations about what should happen have not been fulfilled. Thus there is no specific 'problem', and the 'leader' clearly chooses not to lead in any obvious sense.

The discomfort will in all likelihood exist even for those people who 'know' what is going to happen because of what they have read or heard; and that discomfort exists for most trainers, even if they have 'been there' many times before. The reader of this book may be able to test this notion for himself, if he has not yet been in a T-group. In any event, the following sequence often takes place early in a T-group: group members become uncomfortable because a power vacuum has been created and they are living in a situation that is, as they see it, structureless. The human organism needs some sort of articulated goal and social structure in which to work. The initial behaviour of group members, then, can be viewed as efforts to create the kind of social system in which they, given their present awareness of themselves and their needs, feel they can be most productive.

The motivation for inducing people to become uncomfortable is not sadistic. Rather, the motive is that some (but not too much) discomfort is both a byproduct of, and a necessary ingredient for, social and individual change. And that is what sensitivity training and T-groups are all about. T-groups start the way they do because the overall design calls for people to build from the ground up, in the development of their minisociety. In the process, members must call on their resources, some of which they did not even know existed, in order to create the kind of social and emotional environment which will be satisfying while they learn within it.

The onset of this apparently structureless and goalless condition in a T-group triggers, often in subtle ways, individual concern with problems that tend to be submerged in most of day-to-day life. These are problems of:

* identity ('Who am I and how am I seen in this group?');
* power and influence ('How much can I influence or be influenced?');
* goals and needs ('Will my needs be met and how will they fit the needs of others?');
* acceptance and intimacy ('How close and intimate will I be called on to be and will I be adequate to these demands?') (Lippitt, 1969).

In most real-life situations these questions rarely get explicit attention at the time they occur, and hardly ever get effective attention. When they do it is usually in retrospect. After a trying day at the office, for example, a person may be concerned about problems of identity, power, and so forth. Typically, however, the issues cannot be really worked out, given the absence of critical actors. In the T-group, or in other group learning settings, working out just such problems provides much of the basic psychic push behind learning about oneself. It is almost as if group members were saying: 'I often can't work through such issues "out there", but such issues are critical for me as a person. And I'm not going to blow my chance to do so in this T-group.'

The central processes and dynamics of T-groups

The way in which a person analyses and interprets reality – indeed what he takes to be real – depends on his frame of reference. For example, one's interpretation of why a university organization behaves the way it does depends on whether one is a member of the teaching staff, administrator, student or taxpayer. These points of view are not mutually exclusive, but each one provides an observer with an anchoring point from which he makes sense of what he is observing.

So it is in a T-group. What observers or participants see happening during its development will depend, for the most part, on their own life experiences as well as their theoretical background. For example, a participant/observer could confine analysis of a T-group to questions relating to personality variables, sub-groupings, communications, decision-making processes, and norm development – to mention but a few points of departure.

Here are six frames of reference useful for describing and interpreting what goes on in a T-group.

Bennis and Shepard: developmental phases

Perhaps the most comprehensive theoretical statement of the ebb and flow of T-group development has been provided by Bennis and Shepard (1956). Their position is that the ultimate goal of a T-group is to develop a mature social system characterized by valid communication between its members. 'Valid communication' refers to a state of group 'being' in which there is understanding and acceptance of members as they are. Trust must be created, enabling people to know they can be open and authentic with each other about matters which are important to them as individuals and to the group as a social entity.

Two major obstacles inhibit necessary T-group growth, in the Bennis and Shepard model. The first concerns authority or power or influence in the group. Since the typical trainer signals in various ways that someone else will have to lead the group, the question arises: who? The second concerns the degree of intimacy and warmth that members wish to experience: how free can we be with each other to share and deal with our feelings about ourselves in relationship to the group and to individuals? For Bennis and Shepard, therefore, questions of power and intimacy lie at the root of social relations.

The different characteristics of T-group members are, of course, deeply imbedded in the process of group development, as conceived by Bennis and Shepard, especially those to do with power and intimacy (Bion, 1948). Individuals are portrayed as dependent, counterdependent, or independent, although most of us have all these characteristics to an extent. Each of us has a dominant emotional set about power, and probably back-up sets when the dominant orientation is somehow ineffective or inappropriate. Some people generally prefer situations where rules are pre-set, the task is clear, and the leader, though not necessarily an autocrat, 'takes charge'. Others tend to want to reject authority (counterdependent). They dislike rules, prefer free-swinging situations, and distrust authority figures. Group conflicts about leadership seem to be fun for counter-dependents, but discomforting for dependents.

Independent people, in this context, are those for whom power is not a big issue in their interpersonal or group life. They are not necessarily better people than dependents or counter-dependents. They are simply able to deal with power issues in a relatively calm manner. For example, an independent is less likely to feel immobilized by lack of leadership in a group than a dependent. Further, an independent would be less inclined to reject the leadership bid of another than a counter-dependent.

In matters of interpersonal intimacy, people in the Bennis

and Shepard model are also seen as having one of three predominant orientations: counterpersonal, overpersonal, and personal. Counterpersonals are individuals who, by and large, resist or even flee the sharing of feelings with others. In a T-group setting, they would be likely to say something such as: 'We are not qualified to psychoanalyse each other.' True, of course, but not to the point. Overpersonals tend to look at a T-group as a potential love-feast, and their objective is to become as interpersonally intimate and loving as possible. Personals are defined as those group members able to handle matters of intimacy and warmth without too much conflict. Their styles are usually defined by a vague but rational criterion of appropriateness so that they recognize and can deal with a situation, for example, which is overly cool and distant. In the same way, personals can see when matters of interpersonal intimacy are going too deep.

The Bennis and Shepard theory, then, suggests that the development of T-groups focuses on the two major phases of concern with authority and intimacy. Each phase has three subphases. Subphase 1, the start-up, is characterized by dependence. Attention is centred on the leader's role, on searching for a topic, on structuring, and so forth. There is a tendency to take flight from the group in the sense of searching for 'controversial' subjects outside the group, thus avoiding here-and-now processes.

In subphase 2, counterdependence becomes dominant. The group 'has failed' long enough, and the issue of leadership becomes critical. Sometimes the trainer is attacked, and sometimes surrogates or scapegoats get more than their share of attention. Arguments develop between the counterdependents and the assertive dependents, most frequently about issues associated with structure and organization. Hence the theme: Do we need a leader or not? Subgroups first arise during this time. Their members have similar attitudes towards authority, and they develop as members seek to work their way out of a common dilemma. Dependents tend to band together, as do counterdependents. Conflict often ensues. For example, dependents suggest that the group break up into subgroups, perhaps because 'the group is too large'. These attempts to structure things are usually shot down by the counterdependent adversaries, who correctly perceive that the group is too large as it *is*, not as it *might be*. Besides, they are likely to resist any attempt at influence.

Ideally the conflict is resolved in subphase 3. Here the assertive independents mobilize themselves. The group starts to develop its own internal authority system. Members ignore the trainer, and sometimes ask him to leave the group by saying, 'We can take care of ourselves, thank you.' Usually, however, groups manage to resolve the power conflict without the symbolic gesture of getting rid of the authority figure.

With the resolution of conflicts over power and authority, so the model provides, the group moves into matters of interpersonal intimacy and warmth. The next step, subphase 4, is described by Bennis and Shepard as enchantment and flight. The group is happy. It has been through a trying experience – its members are feeling good about themselves and about 'their group'.

The overall sense is like a victory celebration after a football or rugby match. It is time to relax after the battle for survival has been won. There is discussion of the group's history and its initial reluctance to engage with each other. The over-personals rejoice in assertively communicating: 'Now we can really get to know each other.'

Such mutual enchantment does not last very long. Work still remains to be done. The work is somewhat tension-producing, as it deals with intimacy. It is not that an 'intimacy agenda' is spelled out, but rather that a sense of what is required just seems to develop.

The following subphase 5 is thus characterized by dis-enchantment, because the old conflicts seem to quickly arise anew, even though this time the issue is not one of power. What was seen as a cosy, cohesive group in subphase 4 no longer seems to exist. Questions about goals, similar to those asked in subphase 1, are raised again. Conflicts occur, but this time they are between the overpersonals and the counterpersonals. It can get confusing: members on the same side in the power issue often find themselves on opposite sides in the intimacy issue, usually without recognizing what has changed and how quickly. Subgroups again form, this time based not on attitudes about power but on feelings about the depth of interpersonal contact that should be developed.

Movement into subphase 6 – consensual validation – is once more triggered by the independents or personals. They are able to bring some measure of reconciling rationality to the confusing situation, and their rationality is usually heard by the rest of the group. A factor operating to help them is that movement into this subphase occurs towards the end of the group experience. It is as if the group members sense they must listen to people who appear to have a firm grasp on what is required both in the group and in the outside world. For all too soon, it will be too late when the learning group disbands.

The last session of the group's meeting is usually very warm. People feel good about themselves and each other. The basis of the feeling is different, however, from that of subphase 4. The closeness at that time is probably related to having won a battle. At the end of the experience, subphase 6, the closeness seems to be related to having experienced each other as people in an authentic manner.

There are two factors to consider in using the Bennis and Shepard model to understand T-group processes and development. First, it is an ideal model, 'ideal' meaning not good, but pure and simplified. Few T-groups function exactly as it prescribes, or even in a similar sequence. Nevertheless, our experience as trainers confirms that the model is viable. It helps in understanding what is happening in a group and to its members. Secondly, the development of the different phases may seem orderly on paper, but actual group and individual behaviour are anything but orderly. There is much ebb-and-flow and this can become confusing, even to the experienced observer. The important problem for both the trainer and the group members is to try to grasp the underlying theme or themes symbolized by what the group is doing as it grows and develops, given that reality is less tidy than even the most complicated and conditional analyses.

Mills: life cycles

Mills (1964) takes the position that the processes and activities of a learning group can be best understood in terms of a life cycle, from group formation to dissolution. This model does not postulate any desired final state of the group, such as the consensual validation goal in the Bennis and Shepard model. Rather, Mills' approach is a descriptive birth-to-death analysis of a group. The life cycle has five principal periods:

* the encounter;
* testing boundaries and modelling roles;
* negotiating an indigenous normative system;
* production;
* separation (Mills, 1964, p. 70).

Each period in the cycle poses issues for the participants, and generates specific activities which result in particular group properties. As new group properties develop, they feed the cycle by raising new issues.

The initial encounter leads all members to question the nature of the group and their place in it. This overall issue engenders activities that are seen as naive activism, disillusionment, and entrenchment. These contribute to the central group property of anomie.

Anomie creates pressure for improvement, and this pressure leads to questions about how this state can be changed to another, more comfortable one. Hence a period of testing boundaries and modelling new roles follows. The primary activities through which testing and modelling take place centre around behaviour that is concerned with commitment, authority, intimacy and work, i.e. what is really involved in the task at hand. The new group characteristic deriving from this activity is a vague sense of goal direction, which gives rise to the need to formulate, through negotiation, an indigenous normative system that will aid in achieving goals.

This period of norm development raises issues of new roles for the members. Role demands are worked out through the same kinds of activities that developed during the prior boundary-testing period – commitment, authority, intimacy, and work.

Eventually, most groups develop their own system of norms, values, roles, and even a world view, which leads to a period of production in the form of intense communication. The primary activities of this period are observation, emotional expression, interpretation, formulation, and testing. That is, group members concentrate on their internal processes. Having tried to produce something of lasting value, having learned some important things, the group '. . . emerges disillusioned and less ambitious but intellectually keener' (Mills, 1964, p. 78).

The final period, fed by this productive but limited effort, is separation. The issues here involve holding on and letting go. The activities are, once more, work, intimacy, authority and commitment. And what emerges, of course, is the particular way one specific system dies.

The great value of Mills' approach is its sense of action-reaction-action in the systemic development of a group. Issues affect people who engage in activities that give rise to new group properties that raise new issues, in a cyclical and developmental sequence.

Rogers: personal and interpersonal dynamics

Rogers' (1970, chapter 2) ideas about the dynamics of a developing learning group depart sharply from those of Bennis and Shepard, and Mills. Rogers focuses almost totally on personal and interpersonal matters, and neglects the group as a social organism. His interest is not to build a theoretical model of group life, but simply to describe a sequence of events that he has observed occurring in many groups. These events are, in order:

* Milling around. People start by establishing their own psychological places and roles in their group. This can be upsetting.
* Resistance to personal expression and exploration. At this time the unfamiliar is strongly resisted.
* Description of past feelings. As a way of legitimating

discussion of feelings, group members talk about their reactions to there-and-then situations.

* Expression of negative feeling. This tends to be a reaction to the apparent lack of group productivity. The negativism is expressed towards either other group members or the trainer.
* Expression and exploration of personally meaningful material. As no catastrophe developed from the preceding negativism, a climate of trust and freedom to risk oneself begins to develop.
* The expression of immediate interpersonal feelings in the group. In a quite unplanned way, the expression of feelings begins to refer to here-and-now relationships.
* The development of a healing capacity in the group. The basic humanity of people becomes overt as they offer support and understanding to each other.
* Self-acceptance and the beginning of change. The healing behaviour of the group allows people to accept what they are as a prelude to change, if they wish it.
* The cracking of façades. Group pressures are put on members who have not revealed themselves to do so.
* The expression of positive feelings and closeness. This results as the climate becomes more accepting, and as more members participate at more revealing levels.

These events are seen by Rogers as developmental and natural. They happen because that is what people do in a group, given a non-directive mode of leadership. Further, as these events occur they produce basic encounters. Rogers (1970, p. 33) explains that '. . . individuals come into much closer and more direct contact with each other than is customary in ordinary life. This appears to be one of the most central, intense, and change-producing aspects of group experience.'

Rogers' preoccupation is therefore with personal and interpersonal behaviour, not the group as a social system. Personal learnings about self-group or self-organization do not have a high priority: the group is simply the medium through which a basic encounter may be engendered, thus enhancing self–self or self–other learning potential.[1]

Struggle for membership and acceptance

Another useful way to make sense of what occurs in a T-group is to look at the substantial energy usually devoted by members to answering the question: 'What does it take to be a member of this group?' Few group members ask the question so directly. Usually, it is shown indirectly by behaviour such as withdrawal, expressions of frustration, pairing, and so forth.

An analysis of the membership phenomenon goes somewhat as follows: in almost all natural groups, status and role are quickly established. The goals and behavioural norms tend to be visible and we know what we must do in order to gain the kind of group membership and acceptance we desire, whether in the family, school or college classrooms, in work groups, or social groups. For example, students quickly discover what they should do to be valued by a teacher, even though such conduct may conflict with behaviour deemed desirable by other students. The student has to choose the group to which he wants to belong – the teacher's or that of his peers.

In a T-group, however, the question of what kinds of behaviour will produce the best results is an open one, requiring continual re-examination. This re-examination needs to take place in the light of the developmental phases of the group. Behaviour that is appropriate at one time and therefore wins approval, may be very different from behaviour suitable at later stages of group development. The authors often have observed that dependent participants were 'in' during the first meetings of a group, but lost status and were 'out' as the group moved through a phase of rejection of dependent behaviour.

This does not mean that T-groups punish people who do not conform, though elements of reward and punishment certainly do develop in T-groups. The point is, however, that such

1. Rogers also takes note of other activities that are not as clearly sequential as those mentioned. They include feedback, confrontation, and helping relationships that develop outside the group.

behaviour occurs in any group when a member violates a behavioural, attitudinal, or ideological norm which is important for the group at a particular moment in time. The great difference between what occurs in a T-group and most other groups under these conditions is that the behaviour in question and the reactions of other members to it become grist for the mill: it becomes possible to look at and try to understand the situation rather than to ignore it. The end result of this analytical and diagnostic process is usually that the group members acquire a greater sensitivity for the meaning of individual differences, thus broadening the range of behaviour the group will accept and value. Getting to this point does run a risk, but the risk is usually not a great one.

This last observation needs further emphasis because it relates the issue of group membership directly to the learning goals of a T-group. Note that no particular quality of membership behaviour is 'better' than another during the course of T-group development. Of course, a person who feels highly attracted and involved will probably help the group deal with its problems more productively than a person who is uninvolved or repelled by the group. But a critical moment of learning occurs in most T-groups when its members come to realize that everyone cannot have the same quality of membership. They see that everyone cannot be equally attracted to the group. Some people can be followers, some people can be rebels, and some can be both from time to time. The central learning – simple to write, difficult to actually follow – is that each group needs a host of different person-to-group relationships from which its members can learn and through whose inputs it can develop.

For the individual, the point is somewhat similar, and involves a cost-benefit analysis. That is, if a person chooses to involve himself fully in a group's work, he will have a better chance of personal learning. But it will cost something, at least in the sense of assuming responsibility and sharing of self. Likewise, if a member opts for psychological non-membership, the costs will not be as high but the learning potential almost certainly will be less. In any event, the crux of the matter is to understand the nature of the membership phenomenon and the dilemma it creates for the individual and the group as a system. From dealing with the dilemma, group members can become freer to be what they are and might become, and let others do the same.

Enlarging areas of communicative freedom

Another frame of reference which seems helpful as a tool for understanding T-group dynamics is that what occurs is a continuous struggle, although not necessarily a fight, by group members to establish a social climate with a high degree of communicative freedom. Critical dimensions of such a climate are:

* People are free to acknowledge *ownership* of their ideas *and* feelings. That is, a person becomes aware of himself as a person, both cognitively and emotionally, and does not need to deny his thoughts and feelings because they may be unpopular.
* People are free to be *open* with each other about how they are thinking and feeling about themselves, the behaviour of others, and what is going on in the group.
* The interpersonal and group *trust* level is high. People know, for example, that they can trust each other to say what they mean, not to play games.
* The interpersonal and group *risk* level is low. A person does not have to fear ridicule or ostracization if he does something foolish or violates a group norm (Golembiewski and Blumberg, 1970, p. 296).

These dimensions of an open communicative climate are not always articulated as T-group goals. Yet the flow of events, the risks taken, the frequent psychological pushing-and-shoving that occurs, all enable people to become more authentic human beings with each other. The model above reflects what people do to and for one another in an effective group, whatever their awareness of what goes on.

The process of developing a more open climate in a group appears to be a natural one, under a wide range of conditions. Perhaps it is just that most people sense, at some level below that of consciousness, the kind of social atmosphere in which they live best. The movement towards more openness, however, is not an even one, nor is it deliberate. Looking at the Bennis and Shepard phase development model, we see that in the early stages of group life, members tend to be reluctant to deal openly with their feelings about power, particularly as they focus on the leader. Gradually, however, they test the system through low-risk behaviour. As they find they are not punished for taking risks, the normative structure changes from one which initially imposes sanctions on openness to one where authenticity is legitimated and encouraged.

The sense of enlarging freedom to communicate is usefully illustrated by the Johari Window (Luft, 1969, p. 13), which may be briefly explained as follows. When two people meet, a certain part of their relationship rests on information they have in common about each other or about their relationship. This is the Public Arena area in Figure 4. The information that is common may be superficial – you are a man and I am a man – or of some depth – I have strong needs for power and you know I do because we have talked about it previously. Whatever the quality and quantity of the information, it provides the basis around which we can communicate with each other at the particular moment in time.

Figure 4 The Johari Window (from Luft, 1969, p. 13)

	Known to Self	Not Known to Self
Known to Other	Public Arena	Blind Area
Not Known to Other	Hidden Area	Unknown

The area of the window that is labelled Hidden refers to information that is Known to Self but Not Known to the Other. This is information which, for whatever reason, one person has more or less consciously chosen not to share with the other. It is not public knowledge, and hence cannot be discussed.

The Blind section of the window includes data Known to the Other but Not Known to Self. When we say a person 'has a blind spot', we refer to this kind of situation.

Finally, of course, every interpersonal situation includes information of which both the participants are unaware, and this is the area of the window called Unknown.

The Johari Window model proposes that communicative freedom is increased by enlarging the Public Arena through the processes of disclosure and feedback. A person may disclose something about himself previously kept hidden. It may be simple, as 'I get confused by the confusion of the group', or it may be profound, as 'I've thought about what has happened and have come to the conclusion that I really do want to be powerful in this group even though I denied it previously'.[1] With regard to feedback, a person may say, 'Something I've noticed about you is that every time you start to speak, you lean way forward in your chair. It makes me a little afraid of you.' Or, it might be, 'I don't think you're aware that the productive things you have to say get buried. You lose the group's attention because you take so long to make your point.'[2]

Though this process may appear simple, even banal, it is very subtle and elusive, and even foreign to some people. The notion of feeding back information which may have negative overtones is distasteful to some, for example. 'If you don't have anything good to say about a person, then don't say anything' is a wide-

---

1. For an extension and analysis of the concept of disclosure on the interpersonal, group, and organizational levels, see Steele (1975).

2. Sometimes, in the process of revealing what is hidden or giving feedback about a blind spot, some insight develops that was previously unknown. This has been referred to as the 'Aha!' experience and, if it happens, it is usually by chance.

spread ethic. Yet it may be that somewhat critical information about his behaviour is precisely what a person needs and wants. By the same token, most of us believe our business *is* our business. For certain, all of us are entitled to our privacy, and a T-group experience is no exception. But if a person really wants to engage with someone on an authentic level, this requires taking the risk of revealing some of self. What is risked is that the appropriate give-and-take will occur, that the other person will reciprocate.

Gibb: the importance of trust

As another framework for analysing development of T-groups, we emphasize the group as a setting in which the essential task for the individual is to learn '... how to create for himself defence-reductive climates that continue to reduce his fears and distrusts . . .' (Gibb, 1964a, p. 274). These fearful and distrustful feelings, deriving from what Gibb sees as the dominant defensiveness of most cultures, serve as a primary block to the ability of an individual to accept self and others. The cultural premium is on protection and closeness, not on sharing and openness. As a person learns to accept himself and others, he also becomes able to help others do the same.

T-groups, and indeed all problem-solving social interactions, must deal with the four major sources of fear and distrust Gibb (1964a) proposes. They, and the concerns to which they lead, are:

* *acceptance* from which derives a concern about membership;
* *data-flow* from which derives a concern about decision-making;
* *goals* from which derives a concern about productivity;
* *control* from which derives a concern about organization.

To the extent that these concerns are unresolved, behaviour of group members will be cautious and protective. Little exploration or discovery is likely. Group members will reflect many or all of the elements of a defensive climate:

* Unresolved membership concerns will trigger fear and distrust, as opposed to acceptance and trust.

* Unresolved decision-making concerns will be seen in polite façades and cautious strategy, as opposed to spontaneity and process feeedback.
* Unresolved productivity concerns will result in apathy, as opposed to creative work or play.
* Unresolved organizational concerns will be seen in dependence and counterdependence, as opposed to interdependence and role flexibility.

The key to the productive development of the group is the resolution of the acceptance-membership concern. Unless fear can be lowered and trust heightened, the process of developing a defence-reducing climate will be stymied.

The extent to which this and other concerns can be productively resolved is affected by the degree of reliance on two leadership strategies: persuasion or participation. The persuasive model, which is based on fear and distrust, comes into play the more the group is unable to resolve its problems, and engenders more fear and distrust. It is only as group members are able to learn and enact a participative technology, frequently by trial and error, that they help each other grow and learn in a personal, accepting fashion.

Gibb's view of group growth focuses on the critical relationship between the need for reduction of defences and the enhancing of trust in the creation of productive settings for personal learning. Without the development of trust, the chances are that the group will wallow in fragmented and disconnected interactions.

The aim of this chapter has been to present several frames of reference which are of help in understanding T-group dynamics. The approaches and ideas are not separate and distinct from one another. But so much the better. Irrespective of viewpoint, the central issue is that what happens in a T-group can be understood from a variety of overlapping perspectives that are partially distinct. What happens in a T-group is not mystical and beyond description, although available descriptions do need to be made more complex and comprehensive.

5 The Role of the Trainer

T-group participants usually describe their group trainer's activities in very simple terms. 'He just showed up, and most of the time said nothing' is a common early reply to a query about the trainer's role. Other participants may see the trainer as a kind of Western guru.

The trainer's role is both more and less consequential than such descriptions imply, but the discrepancy is understandable. Participants who have a limited view of the trainer probably have difficulty in describing what happens in sensitivity training. The 'teacher' does not behave like a teacher; in fact, he does not teach in any traditional sense. So participants dispense with it as 'just sitting and not doing very much'. Those who see the trainer as a guru give themselves too little credit for the powerful things that go on in the T-groups. Assigning guru status to the trainer can be a way of avoiding personal responsibility for what happens, moreover.

The aim of this chapter is to clarify the complexities of the trainer's role, to reduce the discrepancy between what a trainer does and what he is seen as doing.

The trainer's basic functions

We start with an outline of the trainer's role and activities, based on the four functions emphasized by Lieberman, Yalom, and Miles (1973): emotional stimulation, caring, meaning-attribution, and executive functions. *Emotional stimulation* has to do with the release of emotions by giving a model. The trainer discloses himself, and thus legitimates similar behaviour by participants. *Caring* behaviour is the expression of concern and warmth for the members of the group as felt by the trainer. *Meaning-attribution* is behaviour aimed at helping the participants understand the processes that are occurring. The *executive* function is boundary-setting, managing time, ordering the sequence of events, and so forth.

Not all the trainers in the Lieberman study, of course, give equal weight to these functions. According to the degree of emphasis placed on each function, trainers were classified as: Energizers, Providers, Social Engineers, Impersonals, Laissez-faire, and Managers (Lieberman, Yalom, and Miles, 1973, pp. 242–4). Figure 5 summarizes the emphases given by different trainers to specific trainer functions.

Figure 5 Relationship between trainer type and amount of emphasis on trainer function

Trainer type	Trainer functions			
	Emotional stimulation	Caring	Meaning-attribution	Executive
Energizer	High	High	Moderate-High	Moderate-High
Provider	Moderate	High	High	Moderate
Social Engineer	Low	Moderate	High	Low
Impersonal	Moderate-High	Low	Moderate	Low
Laissez-faire	Low	Low	Moderate-High	Low
Manager	Low	Moderate	Moderate	High

Trainers differ both in the functions they emphasize, and in the amount of activity in which they engage in the group. For example, the Energizers are highly active in all four functions. Laissez-faire trainers, on the other hand, are inactive except in trying to assign meaning to events in the group.

There is no firm evidence yet which trainer role is most effective, and indeed search for such evidence may be ill-advised. The key issue is probably not one trainer's particular style, but the flexibility in adopting various styles as situations and participants require. Different strokes for different folks seems a useful guideline in this regard. Some evidence does suggest that too much of even a good thing can be damaging or tragic.[1]

Differences in trainer style can also be related to different group goals. Lomranz, Lakin and Schiffman (1972) attempted to categorize group learning from the trainer's point of view. Their research yielded three types of goals: (1) The expanding of personal and interpersonal experience, (2) personal and interpersonal effectiveness and learning, and (3) personal and interpersonal remedial experience. Behaviour and intervention strategy differed according to the trainer's goals. Thus, those who focused on effectiveness and learning were apt to be concerned with group and interpersonal processes and communications. Such a trainer might be classified in Table 5 as a Social Engineer, or perhaps a Provider. The trainer who saw the group as primarily an opportunity for expanded awareness was likely to emphasize sensory awareness, expressiveness, and some sort of mysticism in his interventions. Such a trainer often would be an Energizer. And the remedially-oriented trainer most closely represented the group therapist in point of view. Such a trainer – a Manager, Provider, or perhaps an Impersonal – would use the group setting to help members more effectively manage their emotions.

On a more specific behavioural level, Tannenbaum, Weschler, and Maszarik (1961) suggest a classification of several sets of activities in which trainers engage, regardless of their orientation:

* creating situations conducive to learning;
* establishing a model of behaviour;
* introducing new values;
* facilitating the flow of communications;
* participating as an expert.

We shall elaborate on this classification.

Creating situations conducive to learning

The trainer's job is to create situations conducive to learning.

1. See the last section in this chapter which reports data of some possible effects of unretrieved emphasis on the Energizer role.

Indeed, a trainer's very presence in the group contains learning potential. For example, the problem might be: how do we deal with an authority figure who does not behave the way we think he should?

At another extreme, a trainer could be very active in suggesting – or even commanding! – highly-structured exercises. In a T-group which is having problems in sorting out its own leadership, the trainer might ask the group members to rate each other on their degree of influence in the group. Participants would write down their rankings, which are made public on a sheet of paper. Such an exercise highlights what has been going on in the way of leadership. Members then have a chance to talk about how they react to their rankings. They may express frustration with their inability to exert influence, or even their concerns about having been too influential, and providing too much direction of which they were not confident.

The trainer might sense that role-playing would help group members understand and deal with a problem. For instance, if one person finds difficulty in feeding back to another what in the latter's behaviour is helpful or hindering, the trainer may suggest that the two people switch roles, each playing the part of the other. Each gets a chance to see how he appears to the other.

An increasingly popular kind of structural intervention, and a controversial one, is to ask the group to engage in some kind of non-verbal exercise. Some trainers will use non-verbal techniques (NVT) only to help in dealing with a problem T-group members cannot manage effectively on the verbal level. For other trainers, a group experience can be a continuous series of NVTs.

The former use of NVTs is illustrated by a gentle experience during a T-group session with inner-city teachers. Black–white relations were a problem in the group, the underlying question being: How can we get closer together as people? It occurred to the trainer that a black person's hair is frequently an object of curiosity for whites. How does it feel? Is it really like steel wool? So the structuring intervention was: 'How many of you have never touched a Negro's hair, and would you like to?' A number of whites responded in the affirmative and, with the agreement of a black person, touched and rumpled his hair. Surprisingly to most whites, the hair was soft and not at all what they had imagined. It turned out to be a good experience for all and brought them closer together, in many different ways.

The foregoing examples only illustrate a few of the things a trainer could do in order to help create new learning for a group. Some trainers engage in few of these kinds of activities; others are very active. The critical point is that, regardless of the extent of the interventions, if they are to be helpful to the group and individuals, they need to be related to and integrated with the problem the group is working on at a specific moment. What is not helpful is a bag of tricks to be dished out to the group at the trainer's whim.

Establishing a model of behaviour

All trainers can help a group by modelling those behaviours which are likely to generate a productive learning experience. As with any authority figure, the trainer's modelling – whether deliberate or not – is potent for many participants. The effect is much the same as the effect of a boss's behaviour as a model for his subordinates. In large bureaucracies, subordinates tend to take on many of the behavioural patterns of their boss. After all, the feeling is, the boss's position implies that the organization values his style. And, since many subordinates wish to be similarly elevated in due time, they will try to emulate such apparently approved performance.

In a very real manner, then, the trainer communicates behavioural goals for the T-group members through his deliberate or unconscious attempts to model. When the trainer is under attack, he will be careful to show by his own behaviour how it is possible to respond constructively, instead of reacting in a pugnacious way. For example, a trainer may accept the hostility while helping the attacker – and perhaps even more significantly, all other group members – understand that it's all right to attack, that he the trainer can understand the reasons for the attack, or will at least try to get a better understanding of those reasons. Or the trainer may note when something is occuring in the group which makes him feel anger, joy, or warmth, thus legitimating the expression of a wide range of emotionality by others. More significantly, if the trainer is willing and able to be himself, to present himself as a human being open to examination of his own behaviour, he communicates to the group members that they, too, can be themselves and learn from it.

Though modelling can be and is effective in a T-group, it can also have some limiting effects on individuals and thus on the group. Gibb (1964b) perceptively discusses such limits in his paper devoted to helping behaviour. His major argument is that modelling behaviour is a primary way through which humans learn, particularly as children. When modelling becomes the *dominant mode* of teaching or helping adults, however, real constraints on the learner's growth may develop. What may get communicated is: 'If you can just be like me, then you will be all right.' The consequences can be perverse. According to Gibb (1964b, p. 27), 'Dependency is increased, the pupil seldom gets better than the model. The worker tries to conform to the image of the supervisor. Growth is limited.'

Introducing new values

We have established that major parts of the trainer's input and help to the group are often conveyed less by words than *acts*. That is, the trainer's behaviour conveys more impact than his words.

The 'new values' conveyed by the trainer are often to do with the meta-goals introduced in Chapter 3.

Concerns about, and values attached to, authority provide a useful example. Many people see authority figures as potentially punitive, paternalistic, and not to be trusted. This image is part of almost every T-group, especially early in its life. If it becomes an integral part of the values of a specific T-group, the results can hinder growth. Here especially, the trainer will try to introduce a new set of values about authority which the group can act upon if it wishes. For example, the trainer can confront group members with aspects of their behaviour which reflect an awkward concept of authority. The trainer can convey an understanding of their concerns, but also point to alternatives. Through it all, of course, the trainer's conduct must model the new values. Thus the trainer cannot behave punitively or paternalistically, and must avoid playing games. His behaviour is egalitarian, and opens up possibilities of establishing relationships with authority figures which are collaborative and not boss–subordinate oriented.

These new values are usually accepted, at least for the life of the group. For example, they were accepted in one T-group of prisoners who counted their murders as others might count their business successes. The reasons for this acceptance are debatable. Early on, dependence on the trainer as authority figure no doubt helps greatly. Over the long run, we believe the values gain acceptance because all or almost all people really want to respect those values, in a deeply human sense. And most people can respect those values, at least for limited periods of time.

Facilitating the flow of information

Helping people to communicate with each other more effectively is a crucial trainer function, and a trainer must operate at several levels to be effective. He may simply step in to help clarify an issue saying something like: 'Let's stop a minute, and see where we are. There's been so much going on that I'm a bit confused.' Besides assisting members to determine what the problem is, this kind of behaviour helps induce a norm that sanctions the analysis of group process. A trainer may see Person A ask Person B the answer to question X, to which Person B responds as though he was asked question Y. Person C hears B disagreeing with A and becomes angry at B. At such times, a trainer may say to C: 'I don't believe you heard what B said. Could you try to tell him what you heard so we can check this thing out?' Or, the trainer may remark: 'C, I thought I heard B say one thing but your behaviour tells me you heard something else. Maybe we'd better make sure we all heard the same thing.'

A somewhat more delicate kind of intervention can facilitate communication and, at the same time, start to develop norms regarding the legitimacy of being open with one's feelings. Thus a trainer can be alert for double messages that people send each other. For example, during a recent T-group session one member was talking, rather platitudinously, about social problems which result from not being honest with one another. A second member very quickly shot back: 'Where did you read that?' Of course, the questioner was not really asking a question. Rather, when the trainer drew attention to the bite in the question, the questioner confessed: 'That monologue was fatuous and boring.' The point of this illustration is closely related to the goals of sensitivity training. Double messages are confusing and tend to create distrust. It seems more productive, for the most part, to try to be open about one's thoughts and feelings than to cloak them with hostile humour. Trainers can help in that regard.

Participating as an expert

The trainer's expertise is required much less than some group members think, and much more than others believe. Nevertheless, there are usually occasions in the life of every group when understanding current processes and, hence, further group development may be aided by a substantive contribution based on the trainer's experience or knowledge of theory or research. Usually, these contributions take the form of providing conceptual handles for events which have just taken place or are in process. As a case in point, a trainer may observe that a group has developed a particular norm of membership – crying may seem to be the price of admission. The trainer may dramatize the restrictiveness of such a norm by presenting a brief lecture on norms, their characteristics, and the effects of narrow conformity on behaviour. Group members thus may be better to conceptualize their process, and make more deliberate decisions about their future.

There are, of course, many more roles and behaviours in which a T-group trainer can engage. Three that are important are those of protector, confronter, and 'member' of the group.

The trainer as a protector

T-groups tend to be open and loose affairs in which emotion plays a major role. A participant may get carried away with his quest for openness in himself and others. His belief may be that what is good for him must be good for the others, and he may vigorously or even viciously turn on someone who is less enamoured of personal openness. Similarly, there are times when a group majority perceives a member obstinately blocking its development, and their heavy artillery is brought out for a frontal attack on the offender so as to break down what is seen as resistance. For example, as a group moves closer to examining personal and interpersonal emotionality, a member may object to what is going on as an invasion of privacy, or with the warning that 'we are not psychiatrists'. If the objector persists, the group may mobilize itself so as to reduce his options: to agree, or to continue to object and be put psychologically outside the group.

On such occasions, a 'caution light' should flash for the trainer. For the most part, people seem to stop well before they push a person beyond the point at which learning stops. Usually, indeed, most people stop very far short indeed. However, there are instances when it is necessary for a trainer to step in and help a person get out. The trainer may say: 'I wonder if we're aware that you may be pushing Jim further than it's helpful either for him or for us.' Or, more directly to Jim: 'Do you want to be off the hook?' Besides raising the issue directly, and thus presenting the group and the individual with options, the trainer communicates a very important point, that the trainer is concerned about the welfare of each member, and can be counted on to help in times of stress. Trainers of the kind of sensitivity training experience emphasized here are not interested in a communal blood-letting.

The trainer as a confronter

Confrontation here does not have the same meaning as in 'confrontation politics'. The latter usually involves the presentation of a set of demands, often unmeetable and not intended to be met, as a ritualistic prelude to more violent action. In a T-group, when a person confronts another it is for the purpose of helping the other learn about self, behaviour, and relationships with people. A productive T-group confrontation is descriptive, not evaluative. Its specific objective is to communicate to the member what have been the effects of his behaviour on the group or on any one individual. But, and this is an exceedingly important 'but', an effective confrontation leaves the person who is being confronted with the chance to change, while letting him know that he will still be valued as a person if he does not change. This is clearly not 'confrontation politics'. It is not easy to bring off. But it is rewarding when it occurs.

Because trainers are, we hope, more skilful than group members initially, they can early in a group's life help legitimate a norm that it is all right to confront and to be confronted. For example, a trainer may say to someone who persists in flight behaviour: 'Bob, I want you to know that when you take the group into the "there-and-then" I become uneasy. I'm not telling you to stop, but I want you to know what's happening to me.' Most of the time, the flight will stop or at least be talked about. Even then, however, the trainer must face and deal with the question: 'Did the flight stop because I, the trainer, communicated that it should, or did it stop because members realized that the flight was indeed unproductive?' Thus the opportunity is presented for further dialogue and learning.

The trainer as a member

As group members often understand early, a key dilemma of the trainer role involves togetherness versus apartness: are you a member of this group, or not? Are you involved? Are you fair game? etc.

These are difficult questions. The answers usually depend on the trainer's needs and theory of training. Some trainers try from the outset to achieve membership equal to that of the participants. They may do so in a variety of ways, but each usually involves submerging themselves in the group and trying to deal with group problems on the level that the group is operating. Other trainers take an opposite stance. They remove themselves emotionally from the group and define their relationship to it as an outside consultant. They diagnose, interpret, make suggestions, and ask questions, but refuse to involve themselves in the group in a way which might convey any emotional membership stake in the situation. The great bulk of trainers find their positions somewhere between these two poles. At times, they actively engage as group members, then they may move back, becoming more or less outsiders.

What particular trainer style is more productive in regard to the membership question is not really known or perhaps knowable. If a trainer's predisposition is to become 'one of the group', then he probably sacrifices some of the value he could have as an outsider. Conversely, to maintain a rigid outside role may mean that the group loses some of the resources of the trainer as a human being. Perhaps the middle ground combines the best of both worlds. Thus a trainer might derive emotional benefits from a kind of floating membership, if he is psychologically flexible enough, while he also shows by his behaviour that it is all right for any member to define his own role, to be quiet, to drop out of the action for a while, or whatever.

These comments do not settle the delicate matters, clearly. At each stage, each trainer is probably best left to make his own cost-benefit analysis.

Contextual factors and the trainer's role

Aside from matters of personal needs and stylistic preferences, a number of other factors affect the trainer's role and the manner in which he tries to help a T-group. These factors can be thought of as *contextual*. They refer to such things as the purpose of the training, length of the training programme, group composition, expectations of the participants, and the influence of the trainer's peers (Lippitt and This, 1967).

The following brief examples illustrate how such factors operate. The trainer will proceed differently if the purpose is skill development rather than self-awareness. A training programme of three days needs a different approach to one lasting a week. The trainer may be more active in the former than in the latter. A trainer will probably do and say different things if the group is composed of a manager and his subordinates than if its members are all strangers to one another. Similarly, participants' expectations about the training will also affect his role. If these expectations are different from the trainer's, much initial energy may go into trying to reconcile expectations and manage conflict.

The influence of a trainer's peers on his role also deserves elaboration. Most trainers seem to want to learn from each other, to observe and try out particular tactics or training strategies of their colleagues. In addition, as explained by Lippitt and This (1967), there may develop, in a particular laboratory, a preferential norm of trainer behaviour that is taken on by the training staff as the one most appropriate to the situation. Thus a lab may turn out to be predominantly non-directive, or confrontive, or focused on non-verbal exercises.

Parameters of trainer interventions

Of the many questions about trainer behaviour, those dealing with the timing and quality of interventions probably present the knottiest problems of all. Indeed, the only honest statement is: 'It depends. . . .'

The point is that the timing as well as the content of a trainer's interventions are matters of judgement that defy general statement. Sometimes the value of interventions can be doubtful even when the full texture and detail of a specific group's history is known. For example, when does a trainer break a long silence in a group – or does he? When does a trainer try to help a group resolve a conflict – or does he? Should a trainer's interventions focus on personal, interpersonal or group problems? Should he be concerned only with the here-and-now or can he devote some energy to the there-and-then? Obviously, these questions are not directly answerable.

Despite the recalcitrance of the issues, there are some general notions which can put the intervention strategies of the trainer role in broad perspective. For example, Harrison (1970, p. 20) offers two criteria that seem clearly applicable to the trainer. These are:

* interventions should be made at a level no deeper than to produce enduring solutions to the problem at hand;
* interventions should be made at a level no deeper than that at which the energy and resources of the client or group member can commit to problem-solving and change.

To illustrate, a trainer may note that an individual in a T-group is having trouble getting his influence accepted, and then, by inference, diagnose the person's problem on a deeper, psycho-dynamic level than is apparent to the untrained eye. The question is: what problem is the more productive one for the trainer to work with, should he choose to intervene? Harrison's position is that the problem to be concerned about is the public one, and not the one that may be diagnostically clear only to the trainer. Though it may seem that this only alleviates a symptom, that is not the case. A person is more likely to feel competent to deal with a problem that he sees and feels at the moment, rather than working abstractly with some other's interpretation of the problem.

Sometimes even though a problem is recognized by a person who would like to do something about it, the cost of change is just too high. For example, an individual may have developed a style that has some untoward effects but which, by and large, has been effective. To change that style might require the kind and quantity of energy investment that, *as the individual sees it*, would not be adequately compensated for by the predicted change. In situations like this, Harrison's second point suggests trainer restraint. Some testing may be all right; any pushing might be counterproductive.

Harrison's two rules of thumb can usefully be placed in a broader context. Argyris' (1967) position on trainer style and interventions derives from his ideas about the conditions that produce a sense of psychological success for the individual and group, as opposed to psychological failure. Psychological success implies an environment in which a person or a whole group with the help of the trainer, develop and draw on their own resources to recognize a dilemma, to confront it, and test out ways of resolving it. The dilemma and its resolution are the group's property, not the trainer's. The learning that members derive from such a situation is their own, not given by the trainer. Significantly, such personally owned learnings can be transferred to other situations. Psychological success is achieved in a situation where the group processes, and successes and failures belong to the group. Psychological failure occurs when, for whatever reason, the trainer has behaved in such a way that the group 'belongs to him'.

Interventions, then, have to be made in a fashion that permits the members of the group to be their own problem-solvers. This position leads to what Argyris (1971) sees as the primary tasks of the interventionist, whether consultant or trainer. The interventionist should behave so as to develop:

* valid data about problems;
* internal commitment to problem-resolution;
* a climate of free choice.

Given these conditions, individual and group problems may be resolved in such ways that the people involved will be able to apply new skills to new problems as they arise.

Two other propositions are generally applicable to trainer interventions. Firstly, interventions seem to be most effective – that is, they are most likely to be acted on by the group – when they relate to the particular developmental process or norm the group is working on at the moment in time. Gibb (1964a, p. 308) states the point this way: 'The primary methodological contribution that the trainer can make to the group is to express the norms of the group or how he sees them.' For example, it obviously does little good for a trainer to intervene on the level of group intimacy if the group is honestly trying to resolve its conflicts about power. This is the case even if issues of intimacy are submerged in the discussion.

Secondly, trainers wisely respect this counsel: in virtually all cases 'trust the group to be wise about itself'. Times without number trainers have been asked: 'How can you just sit there while all this is going on?' The answer has two parts. Thus trainers rarely just 'sit there'. They observe, listen, try to understand what's happening, and continually make decisions about whether or not to intervene. Moreover, building on Argyris' concept of psychological success, effective trainers need to have a deep trust that people can and will learn how to deal with themselves, others, and the group. A trainer can sit through long periods of silence without saying anything, can let conflict erupt without becoming overly concerned that people will get hurt not because he doesn't care but because he can let people experience a wide range of behaviour and feelings, trust them to be human, and offer help in a way to increase their trust in each other and in the trainer.

Where trainers may get into trouble

Trainers can and do get into trouble with a group, or behave in ways that are unhelpful (Lippitt and This, 1967). The following are examples:

* Being too directive: one of a T-group's most important discoveries is that people can develop a heightened sense of their own ability to solve group and interpersonal problems. If a trainer becomes too directive – in effect, takes over the group – participants may indeed learn something about themselves and others, but they are deprived of the opportunity to 'own' their group. This is a prime condition of psychological failure.
* Providing too much information: similarly, group members often try to seduce a trainer into giving a great deal of information. If the trainer becomes caught up in this awkward situations can develop: once having agreed to provide a lot of information, the trainer will have set a norm about his role which may not be helpful later.
* Being too clinical: T-groups are not therapy groups, and most trainers are not therapists. If the trainer focuses on psychodynamic diagnoses and interpretations or permits the group to do so, the group may move in a direction for

which neither the trainer nor the group is prepared or competent.[1]

* Becoming too personally involved: this has been mentioned previously. A trainer who becomes too involved with a group may lose objectivity, and a good understanding of what is going on in the group. His ability to intervene then suffers.

* Mistaking frustration and floundering for learning: there is a good deal of seemingly aimless activity in a T-group. Much of this is necessary as group members sort out knotty problems or conflicting personal needs that impede growth. But there are times when floundering and its resulting frustration can be destructive. Trainers need to be aware of these times so they can help.

* Forgetting his power: the role of the trainer is exceedingly powerful. Because people in T-groups are at sea, at least initially, they often seek any port in the storm. The trainer needs therefore to develop a fine sense of what he can and should do, of what he can let be and what he should try to make happen. Particularly those group members who are highly dependent will want to gravitate to him for security. Perhaps what is called for is some sense of humility on the trainer's part so that he can avoid having god-like qualities attributed to him.

Trainer behaviour and group casualties

Finally, we turn to the part played by trainer behaviour in the incidence of psychological casualties resulting from learning groups. Research into this facet of group experience is extremely limited.

The only comprehensive study of which we are aware was conducted by Lieberman, Yalom, and Miles (1973), and reported first by Yalom and Lieberman (1971). It was a study of Stanford University undergraduates, and is, in most respects, a model for much-needed studies of other and larger populations.

The researchers defined a casualty as '. . . an individual who, as a direct result of his experience in the encounter group, became more psychologically distressed or employed more

1. See Clark (1962).

maladaptive mechanisms of defense, or both; furthermore this negative change was not transient but an enduring one, as judged eight months after the group experience' (Yalom and Lieberman, 1971, pp. 17–18). Several sources were used to identify casualties. These included information regarding requests for psychiatric aid, peer evaluations, leader ratings, and paper and pencil measures of drops in self-esteem, to mention a few. All suspected casualties who could be located eight months after training were interviewed, either on the telephone or in person.

The total population studied was 204 Stanford undergraduates. Of this number, 104 had been identified as suspected casualties. At the follow-up study time, it was possible to locate 79 of the suspects, among whom 15 were identified as clear casualties. This represents 7·5 percent of the original total and 9·4 percent of the 170 people who completed the group experience. Either figure is far higher than any reported elsewhere, by a factor of five to twenty. Previous studies, none as carefully designed as this, reported casualties of the order of a half of one percent or so of the persons going through T-groups.

The results from the Stanford study also underline the earlier discussion of the trainer's impact, as Figure 6 reflects. Note that groups led by Energizers – aggressive, stimulating, charismatic leaders – accounted for a disproportionate number of casualties. On the other hand, groups led by Providers accounted for the lowest proportion of casualties. It was further reported by Yalom and Lieberman (1971, p. 22) that of the seven casualties that developed in the groups led by Energizers, six indicated that a cause of their problem was having been attacked by the leader. The seventh noted as a cause his having been rejected by the leader. Some Energizers modified their style when they perceived a participant as fragile, but others seemed to play that role to the hilt, as in the seven cases of attack or rejection by Energizers.

There have been two recently published reactions (Schutz, 1974; Rowan, 1975) to the Lieberman, Yalom, and Miles study. Both reactions are strongly critical of the study on methodological grounds. Schutz (1974, p. 7) suggests, in fact,

Figure 6 Incidence of casualties in the 18 groups (from Yalom and Lieberman, 1971, p. 22). The five casualties who dropped out are excluded

Leadership style	Number of groups	% of the 18 groups	% of casualties
Aggressive Stimulation Charisma	5	27·8	44·0
Love	3	16·7	6·2
Social Engineer	3	16·7	17·8
Laissez-faire	2	11·0	12·5
Cool, Aggressive Stimulation	2	11·0	12·5
High Structure	1	5·6	6·3
Encounter Tapes	2	5·6	0·0

that its publication was an 'unfortunate event'. In two reviews of research on the potentially damaging effect of experiential learning groups (Cooper, 1974; Smith, 1975), the authors take a more moderate view of things. Each acknowledges the potential for adverse effects of training but suggests that the incidence is rather small. Nonetheless, both Cooper and Smith stress the need for further research, particularly that having to do with the pre-group experience screening of would-be participants.

On balance, the available data are sufficient to indicate that learning groups are not necessarily love feasts: some people do get hurt there; and people who wish a group experience should exercise caution in choosing the group experience in which they want to take part, and in placing their trust in any trainer.

6 The Individual Learner

Our focus here moves towards the individual participant, and away from the abstraction 'group'. What kinds of experiences will participants have? How will they react to those experiences, emotionally and behaviourally? What will be learned? Or, in some cases, what might prevent choice or learning?

The format of this chapter is simple and direct. A number of common group situations will be presented so that the reader can develop a sense of the human conditions with which a group member is confronted, to which he must react and make choices about, and from which he may learn.

First, a general observation. The kinds of experiences, feelings, and learning opportunities perceived by a participant, as with any other learning, are initially functions of what he or she brings to the T-group. Participants whose life-style includes strong motivation to be open to new experiences have a learning potential probably different from those who compartmentalize experience into a few narrow categories. If events of the past have led participants to place a high value on being aware of and expressing feelings as well as ideas, their learning opportunities will differ from those of the individual for whom questions of emotion are uncommon, scary, or even repugnant.

The kinds of interpersonal and group situations a T-group member confronts are *not* new in the sense that he has never observed or been in them before. What is new is the opportunity to deal with them as a person and not simply as a role-holder in a formal organization. For example, all of us have witnessed or have been actors in power games in organizational life. Our behaviour usually depends on the role we hold in the organization. If we are in the 'grandstand' – let us say, as soldiers in some army whose several generals are jockeying for the top spot – we may cheer one or the other antagonist, perhaps making sure not to be involved ourselves, lest we pick the wrong general to back. If we are unavoidably part of the game, we may deny what is plain to all, or protect ourselves as best we can. Or if one of us is the organizational superior of the players, we may encourage the game and act as referee in the convenient belief that the 'best man' will win. What few of us can do is to analyse such games: to seek to identify the game for what it is, and the consequences it has for observers and combatants alike both as persona and role-players.

The potential in the T-group is precisely to do what seldom gets done well in life. Outside roles are not crucial or even relevant: it is not necessary to *act like* the director of a governmental bureau, an industrial manager, a superintendent of schools, or a teacher! The T-group game involves trying to be what *you* are, behaviourally, emotionally, as well as cognitively, and to react accordingly.

Initial lack of goals and open structure

In part because of its initial lack of goals, as defined by the outside world, the opening sessions of a T-group tend to be rather strange and uncomfortable for most people. It is rare for people to be in a group where they are supposed to do something, to achieve some kind of learning but where at the same time, there *appears* to be nothing to do. Nor do participants have, or so it seems, the foggiest idea about how to go about determining what will be productive. To top it all, the one person who could help most appears to have deserted participants without having offered any kind of usable clues about what they should be doing.

Individual reactions to this stressful condition vary, but one generalization is safe enough. The content of early group sessions is rarely related to the processes which will take place later. Since many anchors are missing, participants often try to convert the situation into one which is more familiar, and therefore safer as well as more comfortable. Some people plunge in directly, in an effort to give structure to the group. 'Let's get a controversial topic to discuss', may be one comment. Others, perhaps finding their position simply too vague, tend to withdraw and say nothing. A not uncommon reaction is for a person to choose to sit in silence, for hours or more. Occasionally the prospect of the new experience discussed by the trainer is exhilarating for a group member. He is pleased to say so. Typically, however, his enthusiasm is not shared by most of the group. Most group members are more receptive to what they already know. Hence the typical early effort to do something familiar and safe by making the T-group like other groups. A member may suggest the group introduce themselves, give their names, occupations, interests in the group, and so forth. Sometimes the suggestion is acted on, and sometimes not. Some members may doubt that such a ritualistic activity will have any real meaning for the group. If a decision, explicit or implicit, is made to 'introduce ourselves', a person may simply refuse to go along even if this means stopping the process half way through.

The first phase of the group's life is the period of highest dependence on the trainer. Dependence can be diversely expressed. A trainer may be asked to repeat his opening statement. Or a trainer may be asked to suggest some topics for discussion, given his or her breadth of experience and learning. As the trainer refuses to take the type of leader role that most people expect, gentle hostility may be expressed, to encourage him to get the message he is so clearly not hearing about being a 'good expert'. References to 'our glorious leader' or 'and do you really get paid for this?' are common.

There may be a good bit of there-and-then discussion in an early group, tending to centre on members' previous experiences, definitions of a group, what a leader should do. Regardless of the content, such discussions can be seen as efforts to avoid the unsettled and somewhat tension-producing here-and-now by invoking a safer and more familiar psychological setting, however laboured the effort.

What happens during this first goalless period often provides the trainer with a pretty fair picture of the way the group will develop and the roles people will play. It is wise for him, however, to remain open to surprises. Sometimes there are 'sleepers'; people who withdraw early but are not quiet by nature, for example. One such type is the dominating autocrat who has learned that, if he is cautious and quiet early on, it will be easier to take over leadership after the initial thrashing around. Or, a person may be playing an activist game in order to test things out when, ordinarily, he does not 'play games'.

Power conflicts in the group

There is almost inevitably conflict over power in T-groups, related directly to the trainer's abdication of the traditional leader role. The conflict may be subtle or direct, but it is usually there.

Group members react differently to competition for power. Some are unabashed and active combatants. Others ally themselves with some central figure in the conflict who seems to represent best their point of view about what the group should be doing. The alliance may take the form of a silent partnership, or it may be overt. For others, the power conflict provides good spectator sport. It is as if they were sitting in a football stadium, not rooting for one side or the other, but analysing the relative artistry of the offensive and defensive moves of both sides. Occasionally, one suspects, there are participants who relish the spectator role simply because, to continue the football analogy, they get a vicarious thrill out of watching some hard tackling or blocking.

For other people the struggle over power can be very discomforting. Consider a T-group in a university setting which met once a week for two hours over the course of a term. Normally, such an experience would not be as intensive as a laboratory group conducted for a solid week. But in this case, for whatever reasons, the group's development had been marked by considerable intepersonal conflict, notably over leadership and goals. The strife had been analysed by the group, with a good bit of learning for most members. The group's last meeting was taken up chiefly with reminiscing. Naturally, much of the discussion centred about the somewhat bitter clashes in the group's life. During the course of this discussion, one member, who had not seemed to have been overtly engaged with the group, said: 'Conflict? I don't think we've had any conflict. We've just had some differences in opinions.' The comment was greeted with amazement by other group members. Most simply could not believe that one member could classify the troubles they had endured as merely 'some differences in opinions'. This person's view of life required that things run smoothly and that interpersonal events be viewed as intellectual matters. Here the participant's life-view failed him by hiding what was so obvious to all others. Dissension over power is not an intellectual matter, its resolution requires emotional engagement with others. For this person, the costs involved in altering his life-views were too great to permit acknowledging the emotionality of the friction. In order to maintain the integrity of his life-style, then, he seemed to deny the existence of conflict. It needs to be understood, of course, that his denial was not 'bad'. But it also can be seen that what he 'brought with him' did not permit him to recognize, let alone learn from, important portions of his T-group's interaction and development.

For the most part, those persons for whom the emotionality associated with power struggles is unsettling tend to drift to the periphery of the group. They wait for the storm to blow over, or they seek others of like predisposition. It is to such sub-grouping that this chapter now turns.

Efforts to sub-group

Much as one can predict that there will be some sort of conflict over power in a T-group, so it can be usually expected that there will be efforts on the part of a few participants to variously differentiate the group in order to 'get something done'. Frequently, but not always, sub-grouping is one reaction to power issues.

Different people react to sub-grouping in different ways. Some people, perhaps those for whom the general ambiguity of the situation has been particularly frustrating, tend to support breaking the group down into smaller units. Such individuals tend to conceive of a learning situation as one in which the goals and methods are clear and have been structured by the leader. Inasmuch as the T-group does not have these characteristics, sub-grouping provides a convenient alternative and perhaps an escape. 'Obviously,' the thinking is, 'what has occurred in the large group has been rambling and unproductive. Therefore, it seems only reasonable to try something else. Smaller units make sense and they will be more comfortable. And we can get something done. Those obstructing progress can have their own wild-ass group.'

Other group members may support the sub-group move because they find it difficult to function in the large group. Time and again one hears a person say something such as, 'I'm not at ease talking to so many people. What I need and like is to have another two or three people and I feel much better.' Some group members will ridicule this reaction, but for the individual so affected it is very real.

Of course, disagreements arise over the question of whether or not to break up the large group. Particular opposition comes from counterdependents, who may view such a move as just another play in the power struggle. Other resistance to sub-grouping tends to come from those who feel that the group must be maintained as a whole because only in this way can it deal with its developmental problems. They foresee, often accurately, that if members structure themselves in smaller units, this step will only serve as an escape and delaying action.

Efforts to formally sub-group do not frequently succeed, although observers can easily identify a number of stable alliances in any T-group. The failure to sub-group is due in part to the idea that most members would like to avoid proclaiming the fact that they 'couldn't make it work'. Moreover, sub-grouping efforts usually take place in the early stages of development, when questions of power are often foremost, and when no viable decision-making apparatus has been devised. The members who want to split up tend to view the failure to do so as more evidence that the group is so ineffectual that it cannot even make a decision not to try to be a group. Those who opposed the sub-grouping feel pretty good. They won!

Expression of hostility

In the early stages of a T-group, numerous overt expressions of hostility may be directed at particular members, the trainer, or at the group as a whole. There are also many times when one person patently appears to be angry, but denies it.

People may have strong reactions to hostile behaviour, even if they are not the target of the anger. For some, to witness this kind of interpersonal exchange is very embarrassing and uncomfortable. 'People just don't behave this way. If you can't say something nice about a person's behaviour, don't say anything.' Similar sentiments are expressed over and over again. Other members of the group are apt to respond, 'What's wrong with hostility? It's perfectly natural. We're all human beings.' The reply to this is, 'Civilized people control their emotions. That's how we get things done.'

At the process level, such situations reflect the clash of life-styles and their accompanying values in the context of the micro-society starting to emerge from the group's interaction. Even as people disagree about the issue of the expression of hostility, for example, they are implicitly developing norms for managing hostility. Agreement within the group defines acceptable outlets for the expression of anger. In addition, members find means of communicating the extent to which they see themselves able to deal openly with hostility.

An anecdote may shed some additional light on the managing of hostility in a T-group. Some years ago, at about the time the civil rights movement was gathering momentum, one of the authors was the trainer of a group containing two black participants. One, Frank, appeared to be very much an activist while the other, Bob, was a middle-class non-activist. Conflict between the two was obvious. On numerous occasions the activist would express his disdain for the other, who declined to respond in kind. Finally, another group member said to the non-activist, 'Bob, why don't you just tell Frank to go to hell?' Bob refused, and as he talked about his refusal it became clear that everything he 'brought with him' to the group ran counter to the way the group thought he should behave. The group's reaction was one of acceptance. No further pressure was brought to bear on Bob because the group understood.

Hostility directed at the trainer constitutes a special case, and sometimes a delicate one. For the counterdependents, ridiculing the authority figure is an exciting or at least engaging exercise. For the dependents, however, showing anger or talking to the trainer sarcastically can be quite disturbing. Their thinking seems to proceed on these lines: 'This group is progressing slowly, if at all. It is frustrating. The only real hope that we have is in the trainer. When things get bad enough he will step in and save us. So, for God's sake, don't get him angry at us or he'll punish us by not helping.'

Lest the reader get the wrong impression, a hostile group is not 'good' nor is a non-hostile group 'bad'. Although anger is as human as love, it is not necessarily 'good' to be angry. If hostile behaviour erupts in a T-group, however, it needs to be dealt with openly to facilitate learning. A primary task for the trainer is to help members understand the target of their anger, and to help focus attention on the specific items of behaviour or attitudes that trigger hostility.

Expression of warmth and kindness

Expressions of warmth and caring occur at all stages of a T-group's development. Concerns about intimacy, however, become more pressing as the group matures and its level of trust grows. It is less risky for many people to express anger than love.

Reactions to the expression of warmth or caring vary widely. For example, comments such as, 'What you just did made me feel close to you', or, 'When you helped Jack just now I felt myself really liking you', can elicit responses that range from an ebullient glow to embarrassed silence. Some individuals positively welcome an overture by another to become close. Others are inclined, both initially and over the long term, to avoid such closeness.

This range of responses to expressions of warmth usually generates meaningful discussion in a T-group. Among the factors which come into play are the following:

* Some people avoid responding to the closeness of others because to do so, experience tells them, is to make themselves more vulnerable to others: the more one person opens to another, the less chance he has to defend himself when the going gets rough. 'The more you know about me, particularly about my needs for close relationships with people, the less I have to hide behind if I need to hide' is a common theme expressed in a T-group. This statement is, of course, absolutely correct. The challenge for a T-group is, however, to develop a climate where the risks involved in sharing of feelings of warmth and liking are low enough not to block their expression.

* Some people do not like to have others reach out to them with warmth because of the implied demand to reciprocate. No problem is created unless the person on the receiving end happens to be uncomfortable, or has difficulty dealing with feelings of warmth towards the other. And many people do, particularly men for whom such exchanges have undertones of femininity or homosexuality. Men, of course, do have genuine, non-homosexual feelings of warmth towards other males. To be able to talk about such emotions is frequently experienced as a new and liberating kind of learning.

* A reason commonly given in a T-group for not wanting to respond to questions of closeness and intimacy is that such discussion constitutes an illegitimate invasion of privacy. It is certainly true, in these situations, that privacy is 'invaded'. The question is, though, when are such invasions illegitimate? The answer is obvious – it is when a particular person says so, even though he generally stands to lose less and gain more than he believes by engaging with another on the level of warmth. Nevertheless, there are times when a person's value system is such that it does not permit reciprocation of warmth. In such cases, T-group members need to learn to respect this value system, even though it may be at odds with group norms, and make room in the group for the individual involved. This process can be an excellent learning experience in dealing with individual differences.

The end of the group's life

Each T-group has a specified ending point. It was not intended to, nor should it, continue on and on. In fact, the relative nearness of the end frequently galvanizes the group to action, even if it has previously been sluggish. Participants seem to sense the need to 'do business' with each other before the opportunity is lost.

A very common response of members to the group's demise is to wonder aloud what would happen to them if they continued meeting for another couple of days, a week, or a term. It is as though many doors have been opened, but some remain shut and people are curious about the rooms behind them. 'Wondering about what would happen if . . .' also postpones the inevitable end of a situation which has produced profound learning and closeness for many of those involved. T-group members often talk about reunions or parties. These are sometimes planned and held, but the effort to recapture the T-group seldom comes off. Which is, perhaps, as it should be. A T-group experience can add very importantly to one's life, but life is not a T-group.

All members of the group, of course, do not view its end with misgivings. Some are eager for it to end, so that they can go home and share their learnings with their husbands, wives or co-workers. Others, a minority usually, have not had a very productive experience. Rather matter-of-factly, they may say 'good-bye' and leave. Psychologically, they may have left the group long before it was formally over.

The setting of the laboratory appears to affect the behaviour of people when the last session is over. In residential situations where the experience is apt to be more intense than a university setting, for example, some people can usually be observed crying a bit, walking arm in arm with another, or just strolling by themselves. Whatever the behaviour, it serves as a psychological decompression chamber.

Closing thoughts

The central learning themes running through the concept of the T-group experience relate to ownership and choice. The more a person shares in the ownership of decisions about goals and structure, the greater the commitment he will have to learning about himself and the group. The issue is one of investment, from which the person can learn about the costs of learning and about the costs of not learning. And each participant is free to make the choice, as well as to learn to respect the choice of others. The importance of this latter point is hard to overemphasize. It involves learning that the decisions others make about themselves are best for them, and that to impose our choices on another is most likely to be counterproductive.

So the process of the T-group constitutes a fundamental analogue of life, though both T-groups and their members all disband. As a participant is confronted with the continually changing dynamics of group and interpersonal life, he must make choices that will affect what he learns. To engage in the struggle for power or not; to become a member of a sub-group or not; to express his anger or not; to express his warmth towards others or not; to engage openly in the talk of the group or not. Regardless of the decisions he makes, his behaviour and feelings become learning vehicles – again, if he so chooses.

What this whole process of open choice implies for many people is a basic conviction, whether they decide to change or not. That conviction is that the manner in which they play out their interpersonal, group, and organizational lives is more a function of their choosing than their being simply victims of circumstances beyond their control. There is the seed of a new humanism in this conviction. This new humanism would involve the creation of environments – work, educational, or family, for example – whose norms sanction and encourage the individual's prerogatives to make choices. Rather than being confronted with an ever-narrowing field of options, a new humanism suggests a field that widens as new information becomes available. The group or organization becomes the servant of the person while still maintaining production goals. It is a difficult task but not an impossible one.

7 Ferment inside the Learning Group Movement

The field of personal learning in groups is not without its critics, among practising scholars and professionals as well as people and organizations that view it from a distance. In this chapter we discuss the concerns and disputes that have arisen among people involved in the field. The next chapter will consider the concerns of those 'on the outside'.

The fact that disagreements, sometimes bitter, flare up sporadically among professionals in any field should neither surprise nor alarm. Indeed, up to a substantial point, ferment should please. For the opposite condition may imply real danger. If the people or groups in any area of human endeavour share total agreement on what they are trying to do and how, their system takes on a monolithic, closed quality. There would be little chance for negative feedback, and opportunities for growth and change would be limited.

The group movement as an intellectual issue

In Chapter 1, which relied heavily on Back (1972), we discussed the growth of the demand for experiential groups in terms of a 'movement' and of pilgrimage. It does appear that a 'group movement' exists. But that movement is protean, with many facets that vary as widely as do concepts of what is to be accomplished in groups. Such guiding concepts are kaleidoscopic, and we can illustrate them only. Thus some in the group movement are missionaries of the faith of 'personal growth'. The thrust of their ideology is that no one can 'be' without experiencing self in all ways – intellectual, emotional, and physical. For other individuals, the movement of which they are no less a part is based on the idea that Western institutions are slowly strangling in their own inept styles of management and organization. The solution to this problem requires developing new ways of relating, structuring, and making decisions which can be learned, basically, through the spread of intensive group experiences in organizational life. Obviously, from the verbiage used, the present authors are more in the latter camp than the former.

Other professionals deny they are part of any movement. For them, their work is much like that of any other professional and scientific field. They have knowledge and skills, and they practise them as does a physician or an engineer. They view the idea of a movement as hampering rather than facilitating the kind of openness that is required for the development of their profession. The movement for them is fad or cult, with a guru-of-the-week flavour.

Three issues

Although it can generate some fervent coffee-break and cocktail conversation, the question of a 'group movement', or several of them, does not severely divide people. There are some issues, though, which have that potential. Principally, these issues are concerned with: the goals of sensitivity training; diverse training techniques, particularly non-verbal techniques; and the qualifications of trainers.

Concerns about goals

Controversy about the goals of sensitivity training centres chiefly about whether or not the aims of a T-group are directed at individual therapy and personal growth, or at training in diagnostic and behavioural skills. Hence the focus is on individual trainers, their orientation towards personal learning, their own needs, skills. The trainer, we have seen, is in a very powerful position. Because of the initial vagueness of the T-group situation, most participants look to their trainer for cues about how to behave. That orientation becomes apparent quickly. Moroever, the kinds of ideas, feelings, and behaviour that the trainer values tend to be picked up by the group, coming as they do from a most influential norm-setter. This influence extends even to very curious, or even bizarre and revolting, cues transmitted by the trainer. Many people have a substantial capacity under many conditions to follow the lead of authority figures – perhaps even a strong need to trust them – a capacity that is frighteningly clear in the description of the encounter group defiled (Chapter 3), as well as in recent experimental work. In one set of studies (Milgram, 1965), experimental subjects were willing to follow an experimenter's instructions even in the face of evidence that other participants might be injured in the process. To be sure, many participants did regret and feel guilty about their actions later. But they did so after they had done as they were instructed.

The late David Jenkins seems first to have publicly raised the question about the conflict over training goals (Jenkins, 1962). He suggests that the original concept of the T-group did not include the notion of 'sensitivity'. The focus was on helping people learn to diagnose group problems better and on training them in behavioural skills associated with effective interpersonal relations and leadership. The first T-groups, indeed, were called BST groups, short for basic skill training. As the field began to attract clinicians, Jenkins observes, the goals started to change. 'Sensitivity' crept into the title, and proponents of skill training were confronted with an unplanned and all-but-irresistible change in direction. That is, the goals of training changed from a concern with behavioural skills to self-awareness. From an emphasis on interpersonal dynamics, Jenkins warns, it is but a small step to a focus on psychodynamics.

Note that Jenkins does not challenge the use of unstructured group experiences for therapeutic goals. Rather, he raises the ethical question of whether this goal orientation belongs under the umbrella of 'training'. His thoughts may be paraphrased in this manner: 'Aren't we guilty of ethical misconduct – in a sense, a breach of contract – if we attract people to training laboratories for the purpose of developing behavioral skills and, after they arrive, they find themselves dealing with processes and problems which, from their point of view, were not part of their learning contract?'

Clark (1962) wrote a rejoinder to Jenkins. He suggested that concern about the training-therapy (interpersonal-intra-personal) dichotomy missed the point. Like it or not, according to Clark, as a group develops it is inevitable that psycho-dynamic processes, both conscious and unconscious, will affect the behaviour of individuals and, thus, the group.

Instead of either/or, consequently, Clark directs attention to the relationship between interpersonal and intrapersonal factors at various stages of a group's development. For example, he diagnoses the early stages of a group's life as involving a fair amount of displacement around problems of authority and intimacy. This displacement reflects the intra-personal base of interpersonal concerns. Clark argues, then, that for group members to learn to deal effectively with here-and-now processes and to gain behavioural skills, members – with the help of the trainer – must try to become more aware of their own intrapersonal needs as a basis for their learning. As this happens, members will become more open to feedback and, thus, better able to deal with their behaviour. They also become more free to view the group in a more realistic light and contribute more productively to it. In short, as a person gains understanding of the genesis of his personal problems with authority figures, so he becomes better able to handle problems of authority when they occur in the group.

Argyris (1968) added to the controversy by arguing that the focal issue is the *kind* of intrapersonal problems that get attention. He approaches the question of training goals from a position similar to that of Jenkins, but does not treat it in ethical terms. He believes that sensitivity training should aim at making people more competent at dealing with everyday life, increasing their personal skills, and making a thrust towards *further growth*. Individuals engaging in such training experience no inordinate strain in everyday life; they feel adequate in themselves, but still seek ways to grow and become more skilful and authentic in their relationships with others. Therapeutic situations, on the other hand, are relevant for those individuals whose orientation is towards *survival* or towards *overcoming emotional deficiencies*. For such persons, coping with daily life is a significant and unresolved problem;

they experience more than an ordinary amount of anxiety about their relationships with others; they deeply need 'to get it all together' before it gets away from them altogether

These two orientations – acquisition of competency and therapy – have important implications for trainer intervention and the development of group activities. In competency acquisition, the emphasis is on creating a climate conducive to psychological success, an environment in which the group members have frequent and ongoing opportunities to:

* define their own learning goals;
* develop their paths to those goals;
* relate the goals and the paths to their central needs;
* experience a challenge in achieving the goals that stretches their present level or abilities (Argyris, 1968, p. 160).

Central in these guidelines is the screening of participants who initially have needs inappropriate to T-group experiences, as by publicity emphasizing their non-therapeutic character, explaining that T-groups are not recommended for individuals under great stress, and so on.

Starkly different assumptions underlie the survival orientation of therapy, as Argyris defines it. Primarily, targets for therapy have needs which differ initially and significantly from those of people engaged in competency acquisition. In therapy, the development of the group as a problem-solving unit is much less critical. The therapist concentrates less on the group, and more on the individual. There is a lowering of concern with the here-and-now and an emphasis on the interpretation of psychodynamic processes, as well as major concern with the antecedents of behaviour. The therapist becomes much more central in the learning process than does the sensitivity trainer. Further, Argyris is convinced that therapy has built into it the potential for an experience of psychological failure, *in the sense that he defines it*, even as it is necessary for certain people. Thus, the conditions for successful therapeutic experience often contrast with those for successful competence acquisition.

A concern related to the goals of sensitivity training,

particularly in light of questions raised by Jenkins and Argyris, has been expressed by the American Psychiatric Association (1970) in its Task Force Report entitled *Encounter Groups and Psychiatry*. The report is not critical of the group endeavour as such, but it does raise questions about the legitimacy of experiential groups when the purpose turns therapeutic and the trainers are not clinicians. The report is quite critical of the many spin-offs which have developed from the 'traditional, responsibly-led T-group'. Taking note of the fact that it is quite possible to evoke strong emotional responses in a group in a short period so that people 'turn on', – the report then goes on to ask, 'What relation does this [the 'turn-on'] have to psychotherapy?' (American Psychiatric Association, 1970, p. 19).

Writers of the report reason as follows: we see a great deal of positive potential in sensitivity training when it is conducted under responsible and trained leadership. We also envisage the possibility of psychiatry as a field learning more about the nature of group dynamics and the potency of group experience from professionals involved in sensitivity training. What disturbs us, however, and with much justification, is the fairly widespread notion that if one level of emotional arousal is 'good', more arousal must be better.

Non-verbal techniques

Questions and disagreements about training methodology, as one might suspect, parallel issues about the goals of sensitivity training. One especial source of controversy is the utilization in a T-group of what are called non-verbal techniques, or NVT

Non-verbal training techniques include a wide variety of exercises, 'games', particular body movements, and so forth. How they started to come into use in training laboratories is not precisely known. Certainly the work of Schutz (1967) and the workshops at the Esalen Institute in California gave widespread publicity to their use. The motive behind their inclusion in training methodology might be explained in this way: in our culture much of the difficulty people have in dealing with themselves and others openly is related to unease about their body and their physical contact with others. Further, we may be able to express non-verbally some of our feelings about ourselves and our relationships with others when, at times, we cannot find the appropriate words. Thus, non-verbal exercises inhibit a person from relying on verbal camouflage, and encourage experiencing sensations that might be masked by words.

Some examples may help clarify the point. Instead of starting a group by stating its purpose and then withdrawing from active verbal participation, some trainers talk for a few minutes about the problems that people have in relating and communicating with each other. Then the trainer instructs that participants close their eyes and mill around, touching each other but not talking. After a few minutes, the exercise is stopped and the trainer asks participants to discuss their experience and how they felt about it.

This simple exercise can evoke powerful reactions. Some people may talk about their discomfort and their reluctance to be close to others. Some may indicate that they liked what occurred particularly, for example, the gentleness with which their faces may have been touched. Still others will speak of having felt quite alone. Whatever their character, participants' reactions can provide an entry point for a T-group to begin its discussion.

Another non-verbal exercise is useful for highlighting the issue of group acceptance and membership. As the group develops, one or more participants may clearly not be 'in the group', they are on the 'periphery of the T-group circle'. Sometimes they are seen as being not very assertive. A non-verbal technique for working with this situation is for the trainer to intervene in the following way: Taking note of the acceptance and membership problem, he asks the group to stand and form a tight circle with their arms around each other. The peripheral member is outside the circle and his task, if he chooses to accept it, is at once straightforward and profound. He must decide whether being 'outside' makes any real difference to him. If so, he is asked to break into the group by any means he chooses.

The manner of 'breaking in' can be most revealing, as can the participant's reaction to the dramatic symbolization of his non-membership status. Thus the outsider's words may not match his action. A participant verbally lukewarm about membership, may sweat and swear to break into the circle and conclude that his words were only protections against acknowledging how much membership and acceptance really mean. Moreover, the reaction of other group members to 'breaking-in' attempts – they can make it hard or easy! – can starkly reveal how they see themselves in relation to the outsider. Often, members will mightily resist the outsider's breaking-in, perhaps minutes after they verbally implored him to really be 'one of them'. Not only outsiders learn from the experience, patently. However the situation proceeds, it provides an opportunity for the group to have experienced membership issues in a direct, powerful and unambiguous way.

These two examples of non-verbal techniques represent a large number of activities which can be used in an effort to enable people to bring to a conscious, verbal level feelings they have about themselves in relationship to others. Such activities can deal with almost any kind of problem occurring in a group. Large collections of such designs are easily available (Pfeiffer and Jones, 1969, 1970, 1971, 1973).

On the face of it, the use of non-verbal techniques in sensitivity training seems not to be at odds with the goals of laboratory education. Clearly, they can help make submerged interpersonal and group problems visible.

Some problems related to the use of NVT, however, stimulate substantial controversy in the field. On the level of the goals of training, for example, Argyris (1967) claims that the burgeoning use of non-verbal techniques is counter-productive. His view is that the primary learning potential derives from the *group* confronting and resolving dilemmas, as opposed to the *trainer* sensing a problem and prescribing the way in which it can be analysed and solved. This position is related to Argyris' concept of the conditions of psychological success or failure. The argument is that the more the trainer takes on the physician or medicine man role, the more conditions of psychological failure develop and the closer training comes to therapy. The group is then owned by the trainer and not by its members.

Proponents of non-verbal methodology are apt to brush aside this argument, their feeling being, perhaps, that what may be lost in ownership is more than compensated by the learning potential of non-verbal techniques.

Another issue raised by critics of the non-verbal mode stems from the obvious emotional power of these techniques. That is, a non-verbal exercise can arouse very strong emotions and bring to the surface long-buried feelings, often to the surprise of trainers and sometimes to that of participants. The question is, then: is a T-group the appropriate place to deal with these feelings that have some potential for trauma resulting from their becoming public?

Related to the possible force of these hidden feelings in a relatively public and non-therapeutic situation is the problem of the skill of the trainer to manage them. Many trainers have had clinical training, and some of them are competent to deal with problems of deep psychodynamic origin. Most, however, are not clinically qualified, thus raising the possibility that they may be asking for more than they can handle if they move in strongly on the non-verbal level. An ethical issue is also involved: When people go to a sensitivity training programme they are putting their trust in the professional staff in charge. Thus, if a trainer, by his intervention, evokes responses he cannot reasonably anticipate, let alone handle, is he not breaking faith with the participants?

Another problem which the widespread use of non-verbal techniques has raised is that they contribute to a concept of sensitivity training as 'fun and games'. The technique may become a shortcut to an emotional 'high' regardless of what is learned. For example, in a laboratory on consultation skills, there was an emphasis away from T-groups towards perfecting skills of organizational analysis and diagnosis. After the first day of the lab, one person who obviously sensed the nature of the laboratory quickly approached a trainer. She asked, 'When are we going to get into some non-verbal stuff?' It seemed clear that this person was looking for her emotional 'high' and was disappointed because she had not gotten it, and the chances of getting it were slim. Another case that we know of (and there must be many similar ones) occurred recently when a college student participant told the trainer he was not doing it 'right', just before leaving the lab. This participant apparently perceived sensitivity training as a series of unconnected non-verbal exercises, and if the trainer was not going to accommodate her, then that would be that. It was.

One related feature of non-verbal techniques leads to a truly worrying problem. Directly, it does not take much skill or knowledge to get a group involved in these exercises. They are no secret. Publications such as Schutz (1967), Pfeiffer and Jones (1969, 1970, 1971, 1973) and others are available in which numbers of these activities are detailed. Thus anyone, skilled or unskilled, can get a group together and start doing exercises. Most of the time, it is probably true that no damage is done. But it is easy to visualize consequences from playing with activities containing such substantial potential for emotional arousal, where either trainers or participants take a casual view of learning with NVT.

In this connection, Pfeiffer and Jones (1969) suggest several guidelines whenever a non-verbal, fantasy, or physical contact exercise is being considered for use in a group. The guidelines are:

* The exercise should be integrated into the total laboratory design.
* The exercise should not be used simply to heighten affective responses, but should be related to learning goals.
* The participants should receive adequate explanation of the goals of the exercise, as well as have time to talk about its impact on completion.
* Trainers who use exercises should themselves be trained in their use.
* It should be made clear to group members that they are free to choose whether or not they wish to participate in the exercise.

These cautions notwithstanding, there is undoubtedly much use of non-verbal techniques by people unqualified to do so, in settings where the restorative and healing powers of an effective group are not available.

The discussion has not been intended to condemn non-verbal techniques, nor to discourage their appropriate use by skilled people. As with any technology, there are costs and benefits (Mill and Ritvo, 1969). But the controversy about NVT is with us, and probably will be for some time to come. Hence the attention here.

Qualifications of trainers

Evidence from a number of sources seems to indicate that perhaps the most critical issue in the field of training at this time is the question of the qualifications of people who call themselves trainers. Martin Lakin writes:

Some people who are inadequately prepared are suggesting to other people what they feel, how they should express their feelings, and interpreting how others respond to them. Some, equally poorly prepared persons, are engaged in applying training to social action and to institutions. Recently, it has come to my attention that there are inadequately prepared trainers who lead student groups on college campuses without supervision. Several eye witness accounts of these groups suggest that highest value is placed upon emotionality and on dramatic confrontation. (Lakin, 1969, p. 924).

The heart of the issue is patent. There is nothing in the world to prevent anyone from 'hanging out a shingle' and advertising as a trainer. The reader of this book could do it, as could anyone who may have been in a T-group and decided they could train as well as anyone else. This state of affairs accounts, we think, for the majority of very unpleasant or non-productive experiences deriving from experiential group training. We observed before that not much skill is required to induce an emotional situation, particularly if a person knows a few rather simple non-verbal techniques. But the mere experiencing of emotionality, however intense, cannot be equated with learning. Such a training strategy may result, instead, in opening up a personal therapeutic 'there-and-then' can of worms that the 'trainer' and the participants may find themselves ill-equipped to handle.

The question of accreditation, certification, or possibly licensing of trainers poses problems differing in kind from those encountered in other professions. In medicine, law, or clinical psychology, for example, members of the profession have the power to control who enters and who does not, often reinforced by some sort of legislation. This power has a long-standing tradition behind it and, of course, is buttressed by the control and certification of professional training programmes, as well as by legal means.

The same may not be said of sensitivity training. Trainers come from a wide variety of backgrounds, including psychology, psychiatry, sociology, management, education, and the clergy. Although trainers could agree, in general, about the desirable qualifications of a trainer, there is no single academic or professional university-based training programme whose purpose it is to teach trainers. It is true that a few American and British universities support departments of applied behavioural science, group dynamics or organization behaviour. And the graduates of these departments frequently become trainers. But there is no approved and accredited programme.

In summary, 'Who is a trainer?' is a question of the utmost importance. The future of sensitivity training as a profession may well depend on its ability to monitor its own activities.

The results of training

Questions and concerns about the results of sensitivity training are continually raised, both by trainers and by professionals in related fields such as management or education. We noted earlier that most participants feel their sensitivity training was worthwhile, that they experienced a new sense of freedom, and learned much about themselves. But the real question is: has it made a difference? The answers are not at all clear-cut, and research is under way to assess changes in both individual behaviour and organizational environment resulting from sensitivity training.

Chapters 9 and 10 deal with the outcomes of training, both

in the T-group and in home environments. The purpose here is to provide a basis for these later chapters by dealing with several general issues.

In a comprehensive review of the T-group research literature, House (1967) takes the position that potentially positive changes in leader behaviour have been observed resulting from sensitivity training, but that potential costs must be considered. House sums up his review with the following comment:

> It has been shown that T-group training is not only capable of inducing anxiety, but that the anxiety is an intended part of the training. Such induced anxiety may have the very unrewarding effect of unsettling, upsetting, and frustrating those subjected to it. The method may also have the intended effect of inducing more consideration for subordinates, less dependence on others, less demand for subservience from others, and better communication through more adequate and objective listening. (House, 1967, p. 12).

Thus, the issue is a classic cost-benefit analysis. The only problem is that it is not possible now to predict with any precision the nature and extent of either the costs or the benefits in a specific case. We are pretty sure most people will learn things in a sensitivity training programme which will serve them well in both their personal and work lives. We cannot define the precise nature of this learning, nor can we be sure that the costs will be greater than the benefits. It is possible to develop substantial lists of *potential* costs and benefits, however.

An anecdote from our own experience will bring the cost-benefit problem into vivid light. An industrial organization for whom we were consultants had decided to test out whether or not to start a programme of managerial sensitivity training as a seeding operation for an intensive programme of organization development. Four vice-presidents had just returned from a one-week laboratory, and a meeting was held with the executive vice-president to decide if the programme should be extended to upper and middle management. The four guinea-pigs had, or so it seemed, learned a good bit, but they were also troubled by what they had *perceived* to be potential trauma. As voiced by one vice-president, 'I'm afraid that the programme might drive some wedges between some of my people.' The executive vice-president, who was scheduled to go to a lab, rejoined with: 'Isn't it possible that it might pull some of the wedges out?' The dilemma thus neatly posed, a decision was made to proceed with the programme. In retrospect, the fear about 'driving wedges' was not supported. On the contrary, many were apparently pulled out. But no matter. The story is not intended to show how 'good' sensitivity training is, but to indicate the kind of issues that must be faced regarding its use.

Still with respect to costs and benefits, it is clear that individual differences can significantly influence the balance. Soar (1966) conducted an extensive study of the effects of sensitivity training on the behaviour of classroom teachers. He reported that an analysis of behaviour before and after indicated that most teachers tended to conduct a more open, less directive classroom after training than before. So far, so good. However, a few teachers who took part in the programme returned to their classrooms only to engage in more directive teaching than they had prior to their experience. An analysis of personality data available about the teachers indicated that 'more directive' results occurred among those teachers who might be described as 'rigid authoritarians'. Soar's interpretation was that such teachers would be inclined, initially, to take a rather dim view of open-ended, ambiguous learning situations which characterize a T-group. Having this bias, they would be more likely than others to see sensitivity training as frustrating and unproductive. As a result, they would be more convinced than ever of the importance in a classroom of a high degree of control and direction – and so, they exerted it. Thus far, less good.

Soar's research does not lead to the conclusion that rigid teachers are 'bad'. Rather, the issue is that not all people can benefit from a sensitivity training experience. It is no panacea for all the ills of our time.

A large number of studies concerning the results of sensitivity training on individuals and organizations also are available. They tend to confirm the impression already given, that though we can generally predict favourable outcomes for individuals, and to a lesser extent, changes in organizational environment, many questions remain unanswered. These questions have to do, generally, with who will and who will not benefit from training, the nature of organizational problems which sensitivity training can help to resolve, the efficacy of particular trainer styles, and so forth. Perhaps it is most important to understand that professional trainers are concerned about these probelms and are engaged in research which may provide some answers.

Not everyone is satisfied with the state of the literature, and some see the learning technology as questionable if not dangerous. Perhaps the most well-known of these critics is George Odiorne. In a paper delivered during a debate with Chris Argyris, Odiorne (1963) presents a number of charges which deserve attention. He suggests, first of all, that sensitivity training has developed into a cult and, in cultish manner, it automatically rejects orderly, rational and conscious criticism. Second, he finds a lack of research results demonstrating that behavioural changes arise from training, and that the only supporting evidence is anecdotal. Third, he asks whether sensitivity training is, in fact, training in any accepted sense of the word. That is, he notes certain criteria of training *qua* training and, from his point of view, concludes that sensitivity training does not meet these criteria. His argument is supported by negative anecdotes taken from lab participants.

There is some substance to these contentions, we agree, and when Odiorne spoke there was even more substance. For example, it is probably true that conversations with people involved in training will reveal some cultish attitudes. One is apt to get the impression that 'it is good because it is good because it is good'. Certainly, this is unhelpful. Odiorne's charges, then, are worth bearing in mind as check against those who see sensitivity training as the road to salvation, as well as a standard against which the reader may judge Chapters 9 and 10.

Odiorne's concern about the lack of research is well taken, but since 1963 much research has been done, although much more remains to be done.

The third point that Odiorne makes – that sensitivity training is not training, or perhaps not very good training – depends, of course, on one's goals and criteria. His criteria for good training include:

* The desired terminal behaviour can be identified before the training starts.
* The course of change comprises logical small steps.
* The learning is under control.
* There are selection standards for admission.
* Results are evaluated (Odiorne, 1963).

These seem to be reasonable criteria by which to judge certain behavioural training programmes, perhaps even most of them. Odiorne, of course, says that sensitivity training does not meet the criteria. To some extent he is correct, as the reader probably will have been able to judge. On the other hand, recall our earlier implication that the goals of sensitivity training are radically different from traditional methodologies of learning and training. Thus, it may be that Odiorne's strictures are more philosophical in nature than empirical.

Finally, Odiorne in 1963 advised businessmen to avoid involving themselves or their firms in sensitivity training until the behavioural scientists go 'back to the drawing board' and put their house in order. To do so would involve, among other things, assurances that trainers were doing training and not therapy, eliminating unqualified people from the field, and focusing group dynamics training on specific managerial problems. More power to him.

Openness and authenticity

How open should the group and the trainer encourage participants to be? How much is too much? A trainer we know once said he was convinced no group was successful unless everyone cried. Is this too much openness? Or is it too little? For us, it is not necessarily either. But we suspect conformity more than openness.

For many people involved in experiential learning groups, their bias is that a person can never be too open. The more a person discloses, the more he or she can learn and the more others can learn. But are there limits? We believe so. Consider the humanistic boundary suggested by Dyer (1972) in his discussion of the conflict between the high value he puts on his own openness and his value concerning the rights of others. Basically, Dyer notes that openness and authenticity cannot be one-way streets. They are the product of an interaction between several people. Consequently, Dyer argues that when the high value he places on authenticity and openness comes into conflict with his values about the rights of others it becomes more important to give in on his individual needs than to violate the rights of others. This is a thoughtful viewpoint, especially when one considers the potential damage that may be done to others in the name of openness.

Stanford (1972) questioned openness on the grounds of the purposes that it serves. He had been in a group that had emphasized openness to such an extent that he experienced the situation as 'phony'. Based on this experience, he offers two propositions. Firstly, openness is usually seen as productive in a group when it focuses on one's weaknesses and not on one's strengths. It is almost as though openness gets equated to and receives approval when it involves a *mea culpa* syndrome.

Secondly, it is more productive to conceive of openness as a means to an end rather than an end in itself. In this sense, a goal of a T-group might be to let people learn the conditions under which they can use their openness most effectively to further group development and problem solving.

Psychological trauma

What is the extent of psychological damage to individuals due to experiential group learning? Is it great enough to be concerned about? If an individual suffers personal problems after leaving a group, did the group experience cause the problem? Or did it trigger an existing problem that was lurking beneath the surface?

From time to time, people in groups have experienced personal difficulties. Some of these difficulties seem to have stemmed from their participation in a group; perhaps most often the group is a setting in which the individual's deep need becomes manifest to self and others. Not infrequently such individuals seek psychotherapy for help.

There is no agreement concerning the number or severity of these occurrences, however. For example, in a review of research Gibb (1970) concludes that there is little evidence to suggest that people need to be terribly concerned about the traumatic effects of participating in a group. The percentage of people suffering adverse effects was miniscule, according to Gibb's synthesis, a fraction of 1 percent of the participants. Lieberman, Yalom and Miles (1973) take strong issue with the nature and incompleteness of the data from which Gibb drew his conclusions. In their study, it will be recalled, 9.4 per cent of the individuals who completed the groups experienced some psychological damage as a result. And such a toll is a matter of strong concern, not to be passed off lightly.

But even if the higher figure is accepted, the issue is not simple. Still unanswered is the central question of whether or not the particular group experience caused the problem or simply created conditions in which it surfaced.

Moreover, the high casualty rate may tell us more about the emotional state of the study population, who were undergraduates at a California university, than about the misplaced potency of the technology. Yalom and Lieberman provide diverse evidence on the point. As we noted in Chapter 5, on one hand, the casualties identified in the Yalom and Lieberman (1971) report were not equally distributed across groups. Rather the incidence of psychological trauma seemed to be related to trainer style. On the other hand, the results of their research also indicated some significant pre-group characteristics of those people who became casualties and those who did not. The researchers describe several of the casualties as perfect candidates for a therapy group, to begin with, or as unsuccessful expatriates from one. Moreover, prior to training, casualties had a lower level of self-esteem and of positive self-concept. They seemed in great need of personal growth, and had higher and (to these authors) unrealistic expectations that the group experience would fulfill their needs than did the non-casualties.

And, finally, the casualties were more likely to use escape to cope with problems of ego-defence, as opposed to one of interpersonal confrontation. 'The entire picture is a consistent one: individuals with less generally favorable mental health with greater growth needs and higher anticipations for their group experience and yet who lacked self-esteem and inter-personal skills to operate effectively in the group situation were more likely to become casualties' (Yalom and Lieberman, 1971, p. 28).

This research, then, certainly adds to our knowledge of potential hazards and the group and individual variables related to triggering that tragic potential. This raises both ethical and operational questions for the trainer. What is his responsibility to the individual? To the group? Is it enough to take the position that the group will 'take care of its own'? Is it wise to trust that a *Lord of the Flies* phenomenon will not take place? At what point does a trainer intervene to protect a person?

We raise these questions not because any consensus exists or is even possible, but for two reasons. Firstly, we seek to indicate some of the unknowns that need to be dealt with by people professionally involved in groups. Secondly, we seek to reinforce the central fact that the process of group training is exceedingly complex and requires as professionals people who are highly skilled, sensitive, and thoughtful about the implications of their work.

8 Discontent outside the Learning Group Movement

Our attention in this chapter turns to questions and criticisms of experiential learning groups that have been expressed by people or organizations outside the movement. Their concerns require careful consideration, and sometimes a response. At other times it is only necessary to note the concern.

Five categories of concern are distinguished here, classified in terms of the basic motivation or source of the concern. We discuss concerns coming from those:

* who see sensitivity training as part of a Communist conspiracy, as immoral, or as quackery;
* seeking to protect privacy;
* emphasizing psychological trauma;
* fearful of group pressure;
* arguing for environmental restructuring.

Communist conspiracy, morality and quackery[1]

Some time ago, a colleague of ours received a telephone call from a minister in a small community not far from his home. The gist of the conversation was: the community was being considered as a site for the establishment of a drug rehabilitation centre. The signs were portentous. Apprehension had been generated; and a community group was investigating the situation with, one suspects, not the friendliest of intentions.

1. The examples and comment we give in this section are drawn from the American scene. They reflect, perhaps, a more striking political-emotional extreme than is evident in other countries where similar points of view may be expressed more subtly. Their inclusion here should be taken to illustrate rather than define a particular type of reaction to group training experience.

One public meeting had already been held in an effort to provide information about the programme of the proposed facility. In the course of the investigation, it was revealed that part of the rehabilitation programme would involve sensitivity training, however that would be defined. It was learned subsequently that one woman had been told that sensitivity training meant people sitting in a circle and shouting and swearing at each other. Because no one seemed to know what sensitivity training was, a member of the investigating group volunteered to get some information. The resource contacted was the organization known as MOTOREDE – the acronym for Movement to Restore Decency. MOTOREDE, though officially apolitical, tends to throw its support to causes associated with far-right political views.

The minister wanted to know if our colleague could come to a public meeting at which the MOTOREDE representatives were to speak. If the opportunity was taken, the minister suggested, perhaps people could be helped to understand sensitivity training from a professional point of view. He made clear that he was concerned about the meeting and that he foresaw a brainwashing attempt by MOTOREDE. The invitation was accepted.

There were about 150 people present at the meeting, including teachers, and high school students. Two members of MOTOREDE were introduced by the chairman of the community investigating committee. One of them spoke briefly about the format of the meeting. It was to consist of a film strip about sensitivity training, and a speech by each of the men. Questions from the audience would follow. The speaker's very obvious implication was that after viewing the film strip and listening to the talks, the audience would be convinced that sensitivity training was evil and that the community should reject any activity or organization involved in it.

The film strip was technically very well done. It contained two major messages. The first was that sensitivity training is concerned with sex and nudity. Cartoons flashed on the screen. One showed a group of people huddled under a blanket with both outer- and under-clothes strewn outside the blanket

Another showed several naked men and women sitting together.

The second message, and it was by no means subtle, was that sensitivity training was another extension of an all-pervasive, subversive, Communist-inspired conspiracy to undermine the morals of American society. Sensitivity training was pictured as supporting drug abuse, student revolt on college campuses, and sex education.

After the film strip had been run, each of the two MOTOREDE representatives supported the messages conveyed by the film strip, with embellishments including the names and activities of some of the major 'villains' in the whole sordid plot. They did concede that it was necessary to differentiate between sensitivity training and bona fide group therapy, with which they had no quarrel. The key to the difference was this: In sensitivity training people engaged in public criticism of each other, while in group therapy they did not. The abhorrence of public criticism has its apparent referent in the 'brainwashing' techniques with which the Chinese Communists attempted to change attitudes of American prisoners-of-war in Korea. The burden of the two speeches was that the interests of the community would be best served by rejecting any programme no matter how well-intentioned, of which sensitivity training was a part.

The reaction of the audience was split, but decisive. Students and some of the teachers hooted and made fun of the film strip and the speakers. Most of the adult community members seemed to be impressed, and applauded. Our colleague did manage, not without some difficulty, to say a few words, none of which changed matters very much.

As many of the readers of this book may know, the daily newspapers and some magazines have featured critical articles and comments about sensitivity training whose general tone can be briefly illustrated. Consider the article 'Hate therapy' by Allen (1968), himself a participant in a marathon T-group. He defines sensitivity training as '. . . a concept in which Leftist behavioral scientists are "merging science with democracy" with *the stated purpose of bringing about a change in the " total system "* [italics in the original] through interpersonal Group

Dynamics in small sessions involving ten to fifteen people. It is, in short, brainwashing' (Allen, 1968, p. 75). He then goes on to say that sensitivity training may be differentiated from group dynamics in its other forms by the presence of self- and group-criticism in the former but not in the latter. The balance of the article – which appeared in *American Opinion*, the magazine of the John Birch Society – repeats the refrain heard from the MOTOREDE group. That is, sensitivity training is linked to Communism, drugs, subversion, and so on.

To a different audience but with a similar argument, Skousen's (1967) 'Chief, watch out for those T-group promoters' seeks to warn chiefs of police. This point of view, first of all, is that behavioural scientists have decided that in matters of civil disturbance, drug addiction, and so forth, it is the police who are at fault and not the civilians. The police are the ones who have to change, and not those who are violating the law. Sensitivity training, according to Skousen, is the way that the behavioural scientists have chosen to induce change. The idea is to break down deeply ingrained value systems through group confessionals. The T-group process is an effort to do away with individualism by homogenizing people into some sort of face-less group. Skousen also stresses what he sees to be the linkage between Communist brainwashing and sensitivity training. After saying that if the behavioural scientists have their way the basis of the American penal system will be eroded, he concludes: 'At the base of this sensitivity training technique lies an ideological war against the entire warp and woof of the American culture' (Skousen, 1967, p. 12).

Some evidence that the thinking espoused by Allen and Skousen has found its way into the wider community is provided in a news report in the *New York Times* of 8 September 1970. At issue was a programme called the Magic Circle, which was being introduced into the Memphis, Tennessee, schools. The programme promotes '. . . character and emotional development of children through effective interpersonal communication and the improvement of motivation and achievement in all areas of education'. It was developed by the Institute for Personal Effectiveness in Children of San Diego, and has been used without controversy in schools in California and New Mexico. Essentially, ten or twelve children sit in a circle for a brief period daily and seek to explore how their behaviour affects others so they can understand and give support to each other.

At any rate, so the news report goes, this programme encountered a great deal of resistance in Memphis. In fact, about 500 people appeared to protest against it at a school board meeting where, among other things, it was charged that the Magic Circle '. . . was similar to voodoo and cannibalism'. The Ku Klux Klan added their opposition to a programme, which one school board member said '. . . uses techniques of sensitivity training to turn individualism into collectivism', and which, he said, derived from the conditioning work done by Pavlov, the Russian psychologist.

Another criticism of sensitivity training in education comes from Max Rafferty, former Superintendent of Public Instruction for the State of California. Rafferty represents an extreme conservative view in education, and writes a syndicated newspaper column in which he ridicules what he considers to be senseless educational fads. Thus, in a column entitled 'Sensitivity training' which appeared in the Syracuse, New York, *Post-Standard* on 20 April 1970, he writes: 'Latest in the long line of educational gins and pitfalls is the seductive if somewhat sappy concept called Sensitivity Training. It's designed to make you achieve "self awareness" and it works this way:

1. You show up with 14 or 15 others who are as inwardly insecure as you are. There's a group leader called a "facilitator" whose main job is to egg all of you on to insult each other right up to the point of actual fisticuffs.
2. You walk up to the politest and gentlest fellow you can find in the crowd, and out of a clear sky you accuse him of being a dirty hypocrite, actually eaten up with vicious hate which he's concealing cravenly behind a mask of courtesy.
3. Then you turn to the sweetly smiling little lady with the quiet manner and you tell her to wipe that silly grin off her face because it makes her look phony.
4. About this time, two or three of your sado-masochistic co-sensitizers brand you loudly as a coward and a trickster, pre-

tending a spurious interest in others in order to hide your own deep-rooted selfishness and disregard for everybody else.

5. Finally, the whole sordid, ghastly truth about your innate depravity is borne in upon you and your partners in scurrility, and all of you break down in tears, sobbing great, racking sobs because you've been such unmitigated blackguards all your lives. Catharsis is thus achieved, everyone is happy, happy, happy, and you have at last attained Sensitivity.' (Rafferty, 1970)

As well as making the editorial pages of the newspapers, articles and letters about sensitivity training also appear on the women's pages. 'Dear Abby' and Harriet Van Horne have both had their say on the matter; for example Miss Van Horne's position seems to be that the whole business is a lot of nonsense. She says, for example, 'I'm . . . a nice old-fashioned girl who doesn't take her clothes off in front of strangers' and '. . . my life adjustment may be forever lacking in consequence of never mastering transcendental non-verbal communication. But somehow I expect to survive. And I'll be $300 ahead of the game.' (Van Horne, 1970).

On the other hand, Dear Abby is much more moderate. In response to a letter from 'Concerned Parents' whose twenty-three-year-old-daughter wanted to participate in a sensitivity training group, she advised caution. Her position was that some of these experiences were excellent, but that there were a good many charlatans and amateurs in the field. It would be wise, Abby advised the parents, for their daughter to consult a mental health expert so that he could check on the group and its leadership before she joined.

The charges of Communism, faddism, or quackery might be brushed aside with a laugh. But to do so would be a disservice not only to the reader of this book, but to the people who have expressed their concerns. Likewise, it would not be appropriate to respond with a psychological pat on the head of the critics by way of saying that some day they may understand and accept. That position would demean the humanity of the critic and the intelligence of the reader. So we shall attempt to understand the problem.

A number of factors seem to be at the roots of the attitudes expressed in this section. First, the concerns are in part motivated by the bizarre episodes and activities which are engaged in by some trainers or training institutes. Several such episodes have been reported in the popular press, or perhaps fabricated by it in some cases. A great many people would react negatively to encountering each other naked in what Harriet Van Horne calls a heated 'womb pool', and which she sees as a very distasteful invasion of privacy. Some might view this experience as so extreme as to be understandable only in political terms – that is, a first step in the direction of undermining morals so that social decay will set in, thus paving the way for a Communist takeover.

A second factor which seems to account for some of the politically-oriented reactions is the emphasis in sensitivity training on the group as the primary learning vehicle. This emphasis is translated, or so it appears, into an engine of conformity. Over and over again in the MOTOREDE meeting, for example, the theme was that the sensitivity trainers wanted to make people incapable of acting on their own, to take away the essence of their individuality so that their thoughts could be controlled by some outside force – a Communist dictatorship.

A third circumstance undoubtedly behind some negative attitudes towards sensitivity training is the unproductive experience that some people have had in a training laboratory. Thus we have reports of T-groups being 'blood baths' in which the aim, apparently, was for group members to tear into each other's global personalities. We have spoken with individuals who have been reluctant to take part in a T-group for precisely this reason.

Curiously, reports of highly productive and exciting experiences in a training laboratory may also induce negative reactions. Some time ago we met a college student who reported that one of his friends had taken part in a training session. What the friend had to say about it was so glowing that our informant reacted with disbelief, devaluing his experience as neither real nor worthwhile.

Sensitivity training sometimes cannot win for losing. Consider the case of a teenage girl who had joined a youth group connected with a church. The group went off on a week-end retreat in which *no* sensitivity training was involved. When the girl came home she was unusually excited about her experience, but was unable to tell her mother about what had made her feel so good. Her mother was concerned and disturbed – she could not understand it all. Her comment was that her daughter was reacting as though she had been to one of 'those sensitivity training programmes', and was losing herself in the group.

Related to all of the above factors is one referred to earlier. The air of mystery surrounding sensitivity training, in the eyes of some, makes it ambiguous, to be avoided or feared, and ultimately to be fought. Certainly these are typical reactions that people might have to strange situations, particularly those where the outcomes are unknown and where what takes place is apparently much different from that which occurs in more traditional learning situations.

Invasion of privacy

T-groups deal with the delicate balance between the need to know and the right of privacy. Generally, the laboratory technology for learning implies that we often pay a stiff price – and exact such a price from others – by drawing a line in ways that define privacy in terms of isolation of person from person. But this is not to say there is no such line, or should not be one.

Whatever the intent, some observers see the T-group as threatening that balance by infringing on the right of privacy through over-insistence on the need to know. Back complains: 'The right to privacy is a legal as well as a human right. The norms of encounter groups frequently treat this right as obnoxious, and the social pressure within these groups is to persuade people to surrender it' (Back, 1972, p. 221).

Is this statement fact or fancy? Our experience indicates that Back's comment is accurate in some situations that are basically due to the trainer's orientation. Groups have certainly been convened in which, in the name of openness and honesty, pressures were put on people to bare their souls to emotional voyeurs of brief acquaintance. And stories of these group experiences, by word of mouth or sometimes in print, quite understandably influence people into thinking that T-groups are uninhibited 'blood baths' that succeed only in unwarranted invasions of privacy.

Our position, as trainers, is that an individual's right to privacy needs to be protected. We see no stable definition of privacy, for that can change substantially depending on whom one is with, and many other factors. But trespasses are still possible, and seductions to gain trespass are attempted. Consequently, as groups develop, continual testing ought to take place to make sure that people are not being pressured into disclosures that they would rather not make. While we believe most trainers feel the same way, we also know that there are others for whom a person's needs for privacy are seen as a 'hang-up' to be done away with as soon as possible.

So, the questions surrounding the need of individuals for privacy in groups are real ones, and should be approached with care and dignity rather than in terms of catchy but meaningless encouragement 'to let it all hang out'. People, at times, do get pressured into revealing parts of themselves, and live to regret it. Further, and even more disquieting, such self-disclosure can destroy or shake some very necessary personal defences, and a T-group may not last long enough for the individual to reconstruct these defences. The common wisdom puts it graphically. Such individuals 'come unglued'.

The problem of the potential for and consequences of the invasion of privacy in experiential groups will not just disappear quietly. About all that can be said is to reinforce the words of caution of Dear Abby who urged prospective group participants to investigate what kind of experience is in store for them.

Psychological trauma

Back's (1972) concern with the possibility of a person experiencing psychological trauma as a result of an encounter group is aptly illustrated by the title of the chapter – 'Playing with Fire' – in which he discusses this hazard. We have given attention earlier to the question of group casualties. Clearly the danger is there, and it is probably heightened as trainers and T-group members insist that a person's deep-seated defences be discarded.

What seems to be at least as disturbing to Back as the casualty problem, however, is what he sees to be a lack of concern on the part of professionals with such occurrences, or with follow-up if they do develop. To make his point, he quotes Perls (1969, p. 75), the originator of Gestalt therapy: 'Sir, if you want to go crazy, commit suicide, improve, get turned on, or get an experience that would change your life, that is up to you. You came here of your own free will.'

Perls's position is shared by many trainers, in various degrees, and has many other advocates who leave all choice to the individual even if he chooses to do himself physical harm. Thomas Szasz, the psychiatrist, has made a similar point on many occasions, his belief being that an individual should be restricted only to prevent harm to others. The issue is one of ultimate individual free choice relative to self as opposed to intervention by an outside party, even an 'expert'.

The general point can be honed to a sharp question. What is the responsibility of the trainer if he perceives an individual harming himself or being harmed by others? There are trainers who would point out what is happening, in their view, and indicate the range of choices the individual might have. Other trainers would take a more active protector role on the premise that the person might be unable to make an informed choice at a particular time, when group pressures are great. Such trainers might intervene directly in such a case, by saying: 'If I were a target of this T-group, I'd be scared. I hear people saying that the individual does not matter unless he discloses what everyone wants to hear, when they want to hear it. I for one challenge that principle, and wonder if others of you are as queasy as I am.'

The authors as trainers prefer the latter position. It is a good rule of thumb to trust T-group members, and thus accord them the ultimate respect we can give any human. But it is even better to assess shrewdly when a rule of thumb might not apply.

Group pressures

Janis (1971), though not writing about experiential group learning, makes some comments that focus on the manner in which group pressures may operate to the detriment of members. First, defining the word *groupthink*, he says (p. 43): 'I use the term groupthink as a quick and easy way to refer to the mode of thinking that persons engage in when concurrence-seeking becomes so dominant in a cohesive in-group that it tends to over-ride realistic appraisal of alternative courses of action.' In the same article he demonstrates the dangers of emphasis on agreement and group we-ness, in the absence of norms of openness and respect for potential deviants. Many a group has gone joyously to the proverbial hell which Janis details, even though few or even none of its members really wanted to. Janis explains the paradox in terms of temerity in saying the discouraging word in groups that value consensus and we-ness above all else. Members of such groups, Janis notes (p. 44), are not inclined to raise the ethical question of whether '. . . this fine group of ours, with its humanitarianism and high-minded principles, might be adopting a course of action that is inhumane and immoral'.

Janis' description suggests a 'honeymoon phase', not unlike that attributed by Bennis and Shepard to 'enchantment' stages of group development. This is an amalgam of pride in having developed some sense of identity, and little confidence that this identity can survive any real testing.

In a way, Janis' comments sum up much of the criticisms that people outside the group movement have to make. There certainly must have been many groups that so submerged the individual identity of some of their members in the name of consensus that its members felt a real loss of self, as they joined in group activities that they preferred to avoid. Much of the good and the bad in human affairs relates to the need to be accepted, or liked, or even just protected by the band of people one happens to be among. And because that need can be high, potential members can give up important aspects of their selves to meet that need.

As with other problems in learning groups, this one usually

boils down to the trainer's values and skills. If his view is 'honesty at all costs', then the group members are more likely to pick up the cue and mobilize pressures in that direction. And because of the high needs that some people have to conform especially under conditions of uncertainty or anxiety, they may go along and engage in activities that they find distasteful. But they do it regardless, in the name of a feeling of group solidarity. Thus, against their will, they may join in a display of closeness that they do not really feel. They may cry, when others do. They may urge another member to disclose self in order to help the group be truly honest, whatever that member's concerns or fears.

There seems, then, to be some basis in fact for criticisms of learning groups as encouraging a groupthink culture.

However, there is another side to the issue. All effective groups develop norms, but they need not develop norms and pressures towards unremitting conformity. Groups may be systems in which the highest value is freedom of choice. Hence pressures to 'go along' can become quite secondary. Again it is the trainer, his values and his style, who plays the critical role in helping group members understand and make decisions about the nature of its value system and the pressures that emanate from it.

Experiential learning and behaviour modification

Perhaps the major social debate is that between the humanists and those scientists who would create environments that would preclude human imperfection and conflict. The very title of B. F. Skinner's book *Beyond Freedom and Dignity* (1971a) implies the nature of the issues that exists between proponents of environmental restructuring as a way to a better life, and advocates of experiential learning groups.

The area of contention can be sketched briefly. Behavioural scientists in the group movement tend to put priority on the freedom and dignity of the individual so that he can make informed choices; Skinner says that this priority is misguided, and that only by restructuring society along behaviour modification lines can man hope to create a world of people living together. Skinner's view is that behaviour is *primarily* a function of positive and negative reinforcements from the environment and that the real problem confronting mankind is to understand better how behaviour is shaped by environment. Once we achieve a more complete understanding we will be able to restructure the environment so that desirable behaviours are reinforced and maintained, and undesirable behaviours are extinguished. The development of a technology of behaviour through which this non-conflictual world might be created is made more difficult, moreover, according to Skinner (1971b, p. 37) because '... almost all of what we call behavioural science continues to trace behaviour to states of mind, feelings, traits of character, human nature and so on'.

Skinner's position has attracted many adherents in academic life, as well as among practitioners where behaviour modification has been used, as in mental hospitals where major successes have been reported in socializing patients into behaviour considered acceptable or desirable by the training staff. For example, Harris (1971, p. 33) writes: 'Breakthroughs by behaviour modifiers in the past three years have put them second only to their worried enemies – the humanists of group encounter – as the fastest growing movement in psychology.' The conflict seems to be more subtle than open. The so-called humanistically-oriented professors go their way, and the Skinnerians go theirs, with little communication between the two.

So far as we know, the issue has not been joined in a public debate. But it ought to be. And these few comments try to provide a little motivation for a more intensive comparison of alternatives. Note here only that these major points of contrast are relevant:

Experiential learning	*Behaviour modification*
1 The trainer legitimates certain specific processes of learning; specific goals are left to the learner and the group.	1 The behaviour modifier determines the goals of learning.

2 The emphasis is on participant choice of learning goals.

2 The emphasis is on participant acceptance of learning goals.

3 The group members provide diverse rewards/punishments relative to behavioural choice or change by the learner.

3 The behaviour modifier provides monolithic rewards/ punishments to reinforce behaviour consistently.

4 Emphasis is on the total person, feelings, state of mind, etc.

4 Emphasis is on the 'perfect person' whose reactions are dependent variables, not givens.

These differences, then, between group learning and behaviour modification are stark. They represent different points of view about both the nature of man and a theory of learning. In a sense, the Skinnerian position is based on a survival-orientation. If we don't restructure society along behaviour modification lines man will not survive. Survival is less of an issue with experiential group proponents. Perhaps taking some sort of survival for granted, the question their thinking poses has to do with the manner in which each individual is enabled to grow and develop personally and in his relationships with others.

Summary notes

Critiques of the group movement have several bases. Some are politically and emotionally oriented, while others have their roots in a more sober view of human behaviour in group situations. The following points can be made about these criticisms. Firstly, professional trainers themselves must bear a share of the responsibility for the negative reactions that certain people have toward sensitivity training. In terms of earlier concepts of an educative human relations experience, some of what transpires today is distinctly aberrant. Aberrant conditions engender counter-reactions and headlines. And aberrant people tend to be attracted by headlines, thus feeding the cycle.

Secondly, there is no Communist conspiracy associated with sensitivity training. If trainers are Communists, their role must produce some severe value conflicts in them. For example, the T-group technology leads to a social system that is profoundly different from the Communist model. Thus the Communist model is based on class conflict that leads inevitably to an explosion, while the mini-society of the T-group is designed to release and deal with conflictual tensions before they culminate in overheated explosions necessary for fundamental social change. Good luck to the Communist trainer who, in these terms, must strive to lift himself by pressing firmly down on his own head.

Thirdly concerns about the invasion of privacy, psychological trauma, and group pressures are not figments of someone's imagination. They are real problems that need to be confronted directly by professionals.

Finally it is a moot question whether the future will be best served through the values in Skinner's approach to human behaviour, or through those of the group movement. There seem to be elements in each that can well serve different needs and different populations, despite a central conflict in values.

9 The Effects of Group Training

This chapter and the one following sketch some generalizations about the outcomes common to training experiences, and discuss the extension of such effects beyond the training setting. In essence, these last two chapters explore the kind and quality of linkages between training and everyday life.

This chapter elaborates the basic points that laboratory training varies in its effects and the enjoyment it gives to participants.[1] To begin with, by far the majority of participants report a meaningful experience, or at least a pleasant one. Which? Evidence indicates that only a fraction of 1 percent of all participants report persisting and substantial negative experiences, although a notably higher rate is reported by one extensive study (Yalom and Lieberman, 1971). Potency and pleasure are implicit in the following transcript of the final moments of one laboratory experience. One of the trainers has just finished summarizing what the experience meant to him, and he asks if there are any final words from the twenty or thirty assembled participants. The reaction is typical, in our experience. An observer reports (Todd, 1971, p. 86):

All our faces seem softened. The effect is that men look like boys. At length a voice:
'I'll give you one word: "Fantastic."'
(From the opposite side of the circle) 'Wonderful.'
'Flyin' high.'
'Thank you.'
'I'll echo that: thank you.'
'Thank you.'
'Thank you.'

1. For an extensive bibliography (over 300 references) on research on the effects of group training, see Gibb (1974).

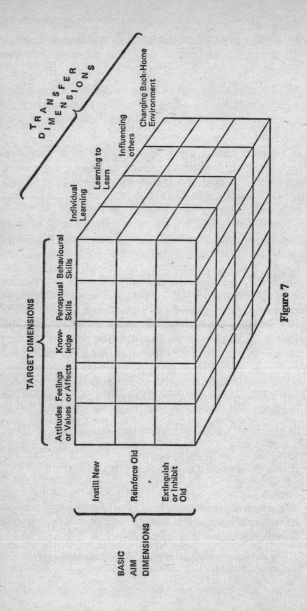

Figure 7

This chapter provides a brief catalogue of more specific effects. We examine the effects of group training from these three perspectives:

* Some dimensions will be introduced along which learning or change can be measured, with the dimensions implying critical questions that should be raised concerning any learning or change.
* Some common outcomes of learning or change induced by the laboratory approach will be discussed.
* Some limits on these research generalizations will be specified, with emphasis on limits of two kinds: (1) not all individuals can or should be expected to react similarly to even the same laboratory experience; and (2) very important outcomes can occur without gross changes in attitudes or behaviour.

Dimensions of choice, change, or learning

Do laboratory experiences generate relatively specific and lasting consequences in participants, in addition to the warm glow of immediate after-effects? It may be said that the popularity of group learning patently testifies that it meets important needs. But any substantial use of resources must face the issue of costs over benefits.

As a vital preliminary, it is useful to detail what qualifies as 'relatively specific and lasting consequences'. Figure 7 provides a useful framework for the critical questions that are implied by the question: What did Jane or Joe get out of their laboratory experience?

Figure 7 approaches this central question in terms of three dimensions, which in effect constitute a complex space for choice, change or learning. These three dimensions can be introduced briefly.[1] First, the figure distinguishes a 'basic aim' dimension, which directly refers to three possible approaches to learning or change, to the 'how'. That is, any choice, change, or learning sequence will involve:

1. The discussion is based on Havelock and Havelock, (1973, especially pp. 47–50).

* instilling something new;
and/or
* reinforcing what already exists;
and/or
* extinguishing or reducing the impact of what already exists.

This list is simple in outline, but reality typically involves a dynamic and shifting interplay of instilling, reinforcing, and extinguishing, singly and in combination.

Second, the 'something new' or the 'what already exists' are identified in Figure 7 as four targets that can be instilled, reinforced, or extinguished by experiences in T-groups. Their focus is on the 'what' of the change process. That is, any choice, learning, or change will deal singly or in combination with:

* *attitudes* or *values*, which define persons, objects, or opinions as variously desirable, preferable, or acceptable;
* *emotions* or *affective states* of the individuals involved;
* *perceptual skills*, which involve developing greater competence in observing what is happening in personal and group contacts, as well as gaining greater confidence in sensing and feeling;
* *cognitive knowledge* or *intellectual understanding* of recurring patterns in human relationships, which is typically reflected in an increasingly useful and complete model of reality;
* *behavioural skills*, which involve acting on the environment to increase the probability that desired consequences occur.

Perhaps the most significant point is that the four targets are interactively linked, a point often neglected in practice. Individual episodes of choice, learning, or change in laboratory education can occur at any one of these levels. But any appreciable and lasting choice, learning, or change is likely to involve all of the levels simultaneously. 'I knew I was a deep lake, emotionally,' one participant summarized his profound learning, 'but I always thought almost all other people were shallow puddles.' In contrast, practice in behavioural skills may seem the most pedestrian target for learning.

This analysis makes no such distinctions between the levels

at which learning can occur. The four targets are interdependent, rather than somehow differentially significant or important.

Third, Figure 7 also distinguishes four loci for transfer. These loci may be thought of as identifying the 'where' or choice, change, or learning, as isolating several important home situations. A judgement about how much an individual got out of a laboratory experience involves separating four related but distinct questions. They are:

* Was the individual able to retain and use in his various home settings, for a significant period of time, any learning achieved at the training site?
* Was the individual able to continue learning at home, by adding to or reinforcing skills, knowledge, emotions, or attitudes? That is, had the individual really learned how to be better at learning? Did the training provide a useful model for learning?
* Was the individual able to help others to learn? That is, was he able to influence in intended ways others in home settings?
* Have any home settings changed as a result of the individual's post-training activities? Or are they perceived differently?

Components of the overall pattern

The four questions above are still too broad for the laboratory approach, and it will take this chapter and the next to develop a framework capable of encompassing the array of effects that need cataloguing. Here we deal with the first two of the questions above, with the last two reserved for the following chapter.

The approach to the first two questions is direct, and it has two emphases. The first is on intent, the second on research.

The ambition of laboratory education is sweeping and profound, and constitutes a severe challenge for any analysis. What laboratory education seeks to do makes it difficult to establish with certainty and specificity what it does. According to Dunnette and Campbell (1968), laboratory education is intended to:

* increase a person's insight and awareness about behaviour in social contexts, by learning how others perceive and interpret behaviour, as well as gaining knowledge of why and how a person behaves in different social situations;
* increase sensitivity to the behaviour of others, by becoming aware of the full range of verbal and non-verbal stimuli, as well as by developing the ability to infer correctly how others are feeling or reacting;
* increase awareness and understanding of processes that facilitate or inhibit the functioning of groups;
* sharpen diagnostic skills relevant in social and interpersonal contexts;
* augment behavioural skills so that an individual can intervene more successfully in social and interpersonal contexts;
* induce a predisposition to analyse interpersonal relations so as to achieve more productive and satisfying outcomes.

Two points relating to these intentions demand note. Firstly, however effective a laboratory experience, there will always be more to do. The intentions are open-ended. Indeed, one major consequence of a laboratory experience is that learners often come alive to how much they commonly miss or neglect in interpersonal and intergroup relationships. This realization can be threatening for some, even intimidating. And for (apparently few) others, this realization of how much they miss or neglect can sometimes be incapacitating. The T-group in a very special way requires that we risk getting information about how little we know or about what we mistakenly believe, as a precondition to adding to our knowledge and skills. The theme is a dominant one in much of our religion and philosophy. To seek to find one's self is to risk getting lost or, far worse, becoming lost. The risk is patent but there is no alternative to risks other than stagnation.

Secondly, these intentions pose formidable challenges for research. Research will for a long time fall far short of evolving a comprehensive theoretical network. Here the research bearing on five themes relating to individual choice, learning, or change is briefly surveyed, to illustrate the impact of laboratory learning experiences. The five themes are not exhaustive, but they represent fairly existing knowledge about the broader range of possible effects, given the substantial problems of any research on group effects.[1]

Change or learning does occur

On balance the evidence clearly favours two conclusions: learning or change does occur as a result of a laboratory experience; and the learning is of the kind intended. A study by Matthew B. Miles (1965) illustrates the evidence. Miles studied a group of thirty-four school principals who had participated in a two-week T-group. Miles' focus was on changes in job-related behaviour over an eight to ten month period after training, and his research was carefully designed. The trained principals were compared with two untrained collections of individuals, which served as control groups. One control group was nominated by the trained principals, and the second was chosen at random. All three groups completed an open-ended questionnaire soliciting information about behavioural changes at work, and the reports on themselves were compared with descriptions provided by at least six of their colleagues.

Overall, the results establish the efficacy of the group training, when the criterion is changes in attitudes, behaviour, or skills that are apparent to colleagues of T-group participants. In sum, the three groups had these significantly different proportions of change:

Trained group	Nominated control group	Random control group
73%	29%	17%

The specific changes tended to be the kinds anticipated. They included enhanced skills in communication, greater sensitivity to the needs of others, and heightened skills for dealing with socio-emotional processes as well as with specific tasks.

Miles' research does not stand alone, moreover. At least

1. For corroborating details, see Golembiewski, (1972, especially pp. 227–71), which this analysis closely follows.

seven studies support his findings, although contradictory and ambiguous evidence does exist. This balance of research led Iain Mangham and Cary Cooper (1969) to three conclusions:

* Significantly more changes are attributed to those who experience a T-group than to untrained comparison groups.
* Observers identify changes that typically include '... improved skills in diagnosing individual and group behaviour, clear communication, greater tolerance and consideration, and greater action skill and flexibility' (Mangham and Cooper, 1969, p. 72).
* The changes tend to last for a year or so, after which a learning fade-out may occur.

The studies reporting these consistent effects are carefully designed, and their results cannot be easily dismissed. Robert J. House (1967, p. 480) concludes:

All of the studies employed control groups to discount the effects of factors other than the T-Group experience. All of the evidence is based on observations of the behaviour of the participants in the actual job situation. No reliance is placed on participant response; rather, evidence is collected from those having frequent contact with the participant in his normal work activities. The source of the evidence is especially important because of the possibility of bias resulting from self-descriptions of participants.

Other data confirm this general pattern, while contributing a note of caution. Figure 8 presents summary data from ten different kinds of 'encounter' experiences, presided over by trainers with six distinguishable styles. Many of the experiences do not qualify as the kind of T-groups described here; and some of the six trainer styles differ radically from the style prescribed here. But Figure 8 does reflect the power of a covey of common approaches to group learning, in what is thus far the best and biggest of available studies. Six classes of general outcomes are distinguished in Figure 8 among participants eight months after training. Interested readers can get full details about how these are defined from the original source.

Three particulars about figures deserve emphasis. First, nearly half of the participants are classified as having experi-

Figure 8 Summary of outcomes of ten approaches to group training based on Lieberman, Yalom, and Miles (1973, especially p. 110). The higher percentage of casualties noted in this table, than was reported earlier in this book, is accounted for by the total of participants in this particular phase of the study

	Percentage of 133 participants	Percentage of 47 controls
Casualties, defined as individuals who 'as a direct result of . . . experience in the encounter group, became more psychologically distressed and/or employed more maladaptive mechanisms of defense'	12·0	—
Changed negatively after their experience, and retained that change over 8-month period	5·9	12·8
Unchanged immediately after training, as well as 8 months later	34·4	63·8
Changed positively after training, but did not retain that change 8 months later	8·3	6·4
Did not change after training, or changed negatively, but became positive changers when tested again 8 months later	11·3	4·3
Changed positively after their experience, and retained that change over 8-month period	27·8	12·8

enced positive changes following one of the 10 kinds of 'encounter', about double the proportion of positive changes in a control population which had no training. Moreover, about twice the proportion of controls remained unchanged over the six-month period covered by the table. Finally, the table implies some high costs of group training, as measured by major and persisting negative effects on participants. In fact, Figure 8 shows a 'casualty rate' that is higher than other available studies by a factor of ten or twenty. Notably, the lion's share of these casualties of the training process occurred in groups with leaders whose styles differed markedly from the style we have emphasized.

The available evidence provides substantial but qualified support for the proposition that a wide range of positive learning or change can result from a laboratory experience. The evidence provides especial support for the efficacy of group-oriented T-groups as described in earlier chapters.

T-groups are potent learning vehicles

Not only does substantial learning or change result from a laboratory experience, but growing evidence suggests that the T-group is more potent than alternative methods of learning. Indeed, the T-group may be uniquely potent.

Consider a comparison of changes following two training experiences – one a T-group and the other a lecture-discussion course – as compared with changes in some untrained subjects. The design was based on data collected six weeks before training and six months after, by interview, from five sources: the person's supervisor, two peers, and two subordinates. The purpose was to determine whether participants had changed after the training and, if so, whether the changes persisted. Figure 9 summarizes some comparative results from an analysis of interview data, which are consistent with results obtained by other means. The comparisons in Figure 9 may understate the case, moreover. Argyris (1965) reports results even more favourable to the T-group.

Whatever its magnitude, the basis of the reported advantage of the T-group technology seems clear enough. That advantage is in small-group dynamics, in the T-group's high levels of participation, involvement, and intense communication. It is in these features especially that Mangham and Cooper see the 'tremendous potential advantage' of the T-group over other training methods for '. . . producing real and lasting changes in attitudes and behavior' (Mangham and Cooper, 1969, p. 54). The two researchers do not take the next step of arguing that the T-group is a sufficient as well as a useful vehicle for change. But Mangham and Cooper do argue that few changes in attitudes or behaviour are likely when participants have low involvement in training activities.

Figure 9 Summary data concerning the impact of two training technologies (based on Mangham and Cooper, 1969, p. 62)

	Sensitivity training (N = 42)	Lecture-discussion (N = 10)	Non-trained controls (N = 12)
Number of observers reporting positive changes	153·5	29	24
Number of observers reporting negative changes	9·5	0	2
Net number of observers reporting positive changes	144	29	22
Number of observers reporting no change	61	27	39
Net percentage of observers reporting positive changes	70	52	36

Listening skills seem to improve

Laboratory experiences seem to improve that most critical of interpersonal interfaces – listening to others. Listening to others includes more than simply being heard or hearing, which may be rare enough. Thus 'really listening' includes an empathic quality, a listening with a third ear, as well as that most significant of human interactions, the true dialogue that implies the connectedness and participation of both sender and receiver in their common humanity.

An impressive array of studies supports the positive effects of T-group experiences on listening. Boyd and Ellis (1962, p. 6) suggest the range and relative incidence of changes in such interpersonal skills in this summary of their own research:

> One of the most frequently reported changes in behaviour for the laboratory group was an increase in listening which accounts for about 12 percent of the reports. By listening is meant paying more attention to what other people are saying, being easier to communicate views to, and so on. Equally frequent is better understanding and better contribution in group situations such as meetings.

Mixed and complex effects on perceptions of self and others

In a significant sense, T-groups may be conceived as replacements for the gift of which Robert Burns wrote: the capacity to see ourselves as others see us. Somewhat more broadly still, T-groups seek to enlarge and clarify the perceptions of participants. The intent is to get participants to see and appreciate more of the richness that exists socially and interpersonally, and to see all of it more clearly than before. The goal is truly mind-expanding.

Research on interpersonal perceptions has proved to be tortuously complex, however, and it is possible here only to sketch some trends in the literature and some points of concern and lack of clarity. Three emphases are required to begin doing the job. However, only a very thick and complicated volume can do justice to the tangled and impenetrable research literature.

Measuring skill in interpersonal perception

A major goal of T-groups involves increased skill and accuracy in interpersonal perception, of seeing other persons as they are and/or as they perceive themselves to be. However, research has been unable to document consistent effects of this kind. To be sure, T-group participants often report having experienced such effects, often as intermittent 'breakthroughs' involving a number but not necessarily all members of a T-group. Moreover, some research has isolated a broad range of expected effects. Burke and Bennis summarize the results of one study in expansive terms. During the course of training, the two researchers report, T-group participants '. . . became more satisfied in their perception of self, moved their actual percepts in the direction of their ideal, became at least by certain measures, more congruent in their perception of others, and came to see others more as the other individuals see themselves' (Burke and Bennis, 1961, p. 179).[1] They also conclude that such results provide 'some support to the claims' of T-group proponents that 'the training group, and the concept of total laboratory atmosphere, is a powerful medium of change'.

Despite similarly optimistic research, however, most evidence is either inconclusive, or denies that such effects result from T-group experiences. As Campbell and Dunnette conclude (1968, p. 91), 'the studies incorporating a measure of how well an individual can predict the attitudes and values of others before and after T-group training have yielded largely negative results'.

It is a reasonable guess that the research yield has been disappointing in this regard at least in part because expectations are unrealistically high. 'Seeing other persons as they are' covers enormous territory and, consequently, even limited effects may imply major learning or change. Consider that:

* one person can become somewhat more aware of another person's attitudes or reactions or feelings, at least some of the time, even if this greater awareness ebbs and flows intermittently;
* more aspects of a person can be made known to others, although the enormous bulk of that person will remain private;
* most members of a T-group can become more aware and more revealing, if only intermittently;
* many and even most T-group members can be encouraged to test more actively and clarify their perceptions of others, to be more aware of their personal biases, etc. This conclusion is based on episodes in T-groups that reveal the importance of the effort even if testing or clarification is very difficult and breakthroughs are infrequent.

1. For opposing results, see Gassner, Gold, and Snadowsky (1965).

Opinions may differ as to whether these effects are significant and, if so, whether they should be sought after. But one contrast seems undeniable. The research literature sets itself a major challenge for establishing the effects of group experiences on seeing others as they are. Thus the research literature often asks: does A in fact see B as B sees himself, or as B is? The list above implies that more humble questions are appropriate and realistic for judging effects on perception, which is extraordinarily complex territory. Consider only one such question, for example: is A more motivated to seek to know B, given that the task is difficult, that breakthroughs are rare, and that the task can only be begun but never done? Only very subtle research designs can answer such a question.

Measuring perceptions of reality

Research suggests that major shifts do tend to occur in how T-group participants perceive reality after training, as compared with before. One approach to investigating such changes solicits two descriptions of some unresolved interpersonal problem at work, one before training and the second following it. T-group training typically has clear effects on the way participants describe and define their problem the second time around. Descriptions after training reflect a diagnostic style that is more consistent with the goals of the laboratory approach. After training, participants see:

* work as more human and less impersonal,
* clear connections between the meeting of interpersonal needs and effectiveness at work,
* personal needs as a more significant part of problems at work,
* less need to lay responsibility on others for problems at work.

The effects are not universal, but they are widespread (Blumberg and Golembiewski, 1969).

Measuring clarity of self-perception

On balance, research indicates that the clarity of self-perception tends to increase as a result of T-group training. David Peters

(1970) reports that the difference between a person's actual self and his ideal self decreased as a result of T-group training, largely due to changes in perceptions of the self. By implication, the group experience gives participants information about themselves that says: 'You are more like your ideal self than you give yourself credit for.' Or that new information might imply: 'You have shown us that you can be more like your ideal self if you work at it.'

There is no absolute victory for friend or foe of laboratory education in the research on clarity of self-perception, however. A number of studies report improvements as a result of T-group experiences. But at least one major study (Gassner, Gold and Snadowsky, 1965) provides mixed findings about the effects of training on self-perception, and several other studies report little or no effect.

Lessening estrangement from self and others

As a kind of *summum bonum* of laboratory education, its underlying theory implies that the self-esteem and self-acceptance of participants will increase. The implied dynamics are both complex and crucial, and involve four central notions that are seen as underlying any individual's interpersonal competence:

* self-acceptance;
* confirmation;
* essentiality;
* psychological success.

The four notions can be introduced briefly: *Self-acceptance* refers to the confidence that an individual has in self, as well as to the degree a person regards self highly. Self-acceptance depends on the clarity of the knowledge that one has about self, that much should be clear. In turn, that clarity is influenced, if not determined, by the quality of a person's interpersonal and group relationships. Of course, an individual may accept a false self, but that is likely to cause problems, at least in the long run.

Confirmation occurs to the degree that others experience an individual as he experiences self. To the degree that a person sees self as different from the way others experience him, so interpersonal competence is likely to suffer.

Essentiality refers to the condition under which a person is able to express central needs as well as to utilize central abilities. 'What am I doing involved in this?' is one way we express feelings of a low degree of essentiality. The underlying concept of the personality is one of many layers, with values, behaviour or activities being ranked in order of their preference. If a person activates low preferences, especially over a period of time, feelings of low essentiality will result. The vernacular refers to 'scraping the bottom of the barrel'.

Psychological success is basically a function of the degree to which an individual can define his own goals or participate in their definition. This direct statement implies at least four emphases. Responding to the goals set by others can generate feelings of failure even when objective successes are achieved. Psychological success is also a function of the degree that goals are related to an individual's high-preference needs, abilities, or values. In addition, as the individual defines paths to attain his goals, the possibility of psychological success is heightened. Finally, attaining a realistic level of aspiration will induce psychological success. The point applies in two major senses. An aspiration level that is set too high can generate feelings of psychological failure, no matter what the actual performance. That is to say, one can fail even while doing quite well. A level of aspiration that can be attained very comfortably can also generate feelings of failure. Thus an 'easy piece' may not be motivating over the long run, in which case failure follows lack of effort. Or the individual may despise self for succeeding in a facile way.

These brief descriptions imply awesome potentialities in T-group training for reducing estrangement from both self and others. In diverse ways, laboratory experiences are oriented toward heightening these conditions, and thus toward enhancing interpersonal competence. Moreover, as the individual thus becomes more secure with self, so it should in theory be possible to relate more effectively to others. Some research implies that such effects tend to occur.

It is possible here only to illustrate one approach to these critical issues of reducing estrangement from self and others.

The point of departure is Robert Kahn's (1963, p. 14) challenge. 'The theory of T-groups implies reduction in prejudice . . .,' he notes, '. . . should be one of the results of a general increase in sensitivity to the needs of others and insight into one's motives and behaviour as it affects others. No research is available, however, to test this prediction.'[1] Irvin Rubin (1967) focused on one aspect of Kahn's suggestion by investigating two propositions: that a T-group experience would tend to increase a person's self-acceptance; and that increases in self-acceptance would have the effect of raising a person's acceptance of others. Rubin defined 'self-acceptance' as a willingness to realistically confront and accept aspects of the self.

Rubin's results imply the expected relationship between self-acceptance and acceptance of others, with one significant intervening condition. Thus self-acceptance increased for 23 of 38 T-group participants in Rubin's sample. Six other participants did not change, and nine decreased in self-acceptance, as Rubin measured it. Changes in acceptance of others seemed less flexible, however, almost as if there were a threshold effect before increases in self-acceptance would trigger increases in acceptance of others. Only those who increased their self-acceptance a great deal increased their acceptance of others. Small or negative changes in self-acceptance were not associated with increased acceptance of others.

Limits on the overall pattern

These generalizations from research are easy enough to fault. Major methodological problems bedevil research on human change and learning, and the available literature has hardly conquered these stubborn challenges. Moreover, in many areas, research has only just begun. In addition, many of the studies summarized above may be criticized in that they do not establish that the effects are unique to T-groups. Matthew Miles (1965, p. 40) provides a useful summary of these and other problems:[2]

1. For some recent evidence supporting Kahn's hypothesis, consult Holloman and Hendrick, (1972).
2. For another summary of the methodological problems with the research summarized here, see Harrison, (1971).

Research on any form of treatment is classically difficult, un-rewarding, and infrequent. When the product of a process is change in persons, the criterion problem is ordinarily a major one, whether the treatment occupies the domain of education, mental health, or social functioning. Goals are vaguely stated (partly because of ignorance and partly, it has been suggested, to protect the prac-titioner against charges of malpractice). Often, it is claimed that 'real' change may not be assessable until long after treatment has occurred. Even if goals are precisely and operationally defined, treatment programs themselves are usually hard to describe ac-curately enough for later replication. Furthermore, test-treatment interaction is quite likely; subjects are easily sensitized by pre-measures. Even more crudely, it is frequently difficult to locate anything like a meaningful control group, let alone establish its equivalence. Finally, numbers are usually small, and the treatment population is often biased through self-selection.

Miles (1965, p. 40) sees such details as leading to a direct con-clusion. He observes: 'Thus it is not surprising that perhaps 95 percent of all treatment efforts go unstudied, and that even the 5 percent typically show serious defects in design, measurement or data analysis . . .'

For such substantial reasons, the generalizations above must be considered tentative. They do reflect what we can be relatively certain of at the present, primitive stage of development of study. There is a formidable amount still unknown.

But it is altogether too easy to be humble in the face of what needs to be known. Compared to what we knew even a decade ago, research now is in good shape and getting better fast. Four perspectives will be discussed to illustrate the point that the ability to present *any* list of generalizations attests to the fact that laboratory experiences have more or less predictable effects, otherwise, those effects could be obliterated by several powerful limiting factors.

Ideal conditions for laboratory learning

In essence, the laboratory method rests on a complex series of 'if, then' propositions which imply a set of conditions for learning. If learners feel relatively secure and safe in a psycholo-gical sense, then they will be able to learn and contemplate change. Such propositions rest on a number of central assumptions about the ability of the laboratory technology to approximate the ideal conditions implied by such propositions. At least six central assumptions may be usefully distinguished (Campbell and Dunnette, 1968):

Firstly, a feeling of psychological safety can be induced in many or all T-group participants in a brief period of time, whether the participants are strangers or share a common history.

Secondly, T-group participants lack interpersonal competence, which they want to remedy when it is psychologically safe. People do not hear what is said, fail to communicate what they intended, have a distorted sense of how they are perceived by others, and so on, often to a sufficient extent to cause them concern. The assumption is that everyone wants to diminish the number and degree of such cases.

Thirdly, under conditions of relative psychological safety, members of a T-group will be willing to enter into a mutual contract for learning. The contract has two main features. Participants should strive to be constructive as opposed to destructive; and they should provide honest feedback and self-disclosure to one another.

Fourthly, despite their individual deficiencies in interpersonal competence, members of a T-group tend to pool wisdom and helpfulness, as opposed to compounding ignorance and vindictiveness. In the case of feedback, for example, the assumption of maximizing assets and minimizing deficiencies implies at least four conditions:

* T-group members will observe more or less the same real as against imagined aspects of the same participant's behaviour in meaningful interpersonal situations.
* Members can articulate what they see and how they react to it.
* T-group members can convey their messages in ways that are not seen as malicious even when they are not helpful.
* What is observed and communicated will somehow involve a more-or-less complete view of a significant aspect of the behaviour, attitudes, or values of the target of the feedback.

Fifthly, despite their individual deficiencies in interpersonal competence, T-group members collectively can provide the resources appropriate to the range of concerns likely to be encountered. At the very least, these resources include observational and communicative skills. They also include warmth, support, and skills in confronting.

Sixthly, a T-group member's behaviour is representative of what the individual is, or would like to be, outside of the T-group environment. As this assumption is met, so do T-group members come to take any learning opportunities seriously, to own them. Meeting this assumption implies the possibility of transfer of learning from the T-group context, as well as the motivation to do so. Without either possibility of motivation, the T-group experience is at best temporary and at worst counter-productive.

The six assumptions above are formidable ones, and not easily achieved. However, the fact that generalizations can be drawn from research about laboratory learning implies that the technique is, even at the present stage of development, powerful enough to induce the required conditions.

Not everyone needs or wants to change but all need to choose and test

The fact that generalizations can be drawn from research on laboratory effects is also noteworthy because an individual can have a very profitable experience, even with little obvious learning or change. That is, the opportunity to be able to choose or test is, from some important perspectives, more central to laboratory education than is actual change.

Consider a hypothetical illustration of the point, one that seems bizarre but conveys the essence of everyman. Assume that a man comes to a T-group with a specific aim. He is a very successful undercover agent for a public agency, and has been offered a coveted promotion at headquarters that will permit him to lead an ordered and secure existence for the first time.

Our man is attracted by the promotion, and yet cautious and concerned about it. He realizes over the years that his success in the field is based on one crucial fact: he not only behaves as if anyone might be his assassin, but he believes that many specific people in fact have such a design. This attitude is useful in his fieldwork, but he is increasingly concerned that his person has grown to harbour far more paranoid suspicion than his role will ever require. Hence his concern about the promotion. Will his suspicions also be triggered at headquarters, where they will probably be far less appropriate? Will his defences ill serve him then although they once helped make him a legendary field operator?

Under a complex cover, the man attends a T-group to provide one test of these critical questions. He soon has his answer. At least four of his fellow group members, he soon concludes with deep conviction, might have 'a contract' on him. Rationally, he recognizes 'this is crazy because I doubt if anyone could break my cover so quickly'. He is not able to shake the conviction, however, and he refers himself to his agency medical office. Soon thereafter, the man is back in the field.

The man represents a broad class of reaction to laboratory experiences, although he clearly is an exotic example. He has used a T-group to test an important aspect of himself and, for most purposes, he remains as he was. Other group members perceive no great change in our man, but he gets what he is after.

In these features, our example represents all T-group members, or at least aspects of all of them. Let us temporarily neglect that all of us need and often want novel insight about ourselves. But, in addition, we need confirmation of aspects of ourselves that we are relatively certain about, and perhaps even comfortable with. No major learning or change will necessarily follow such confirmation. Testing may be followed by a choice to remain as we are. Or perhaps our self-esteem will rise slightly, in that we are confirmed to be observers of ourselves as others see us and thus competent in this critical sense. The following T-group anecdotes illustrate the point:

* A man had come to believe that some of his interpersonal problems derived from the fact that his anger was clear but his positive feelings were hard to detect, and had that belief confirmed independently by several T-group members.

* A woman had a professional role which required broad social and psychological distance between her and most others, so much so and for such a long time that she questioned her ability to develop strong and warm relationships as a person. She proved to herself and to others in a T-group that she still could, although she did not desire or even contemplate change in her behaviour at home.

Such testing does not always have sanguine effects, of course, as is implied by the minority of cases in Rubin's research in which a T-group participant's self-acceptance was lowered. Consider only two cases. Thus we may get information from others that the self we see is not the self known to others. For example, a man believed he was an empathic person and behaved that way at home, but was distressed to learn that he was not very successful in getting in tune with the feelings of others. It can be painful to learn that distressing aspects of ourselves are also distressing to others. This can confirm our worst fears, as it were; and it may be very impactful on us that others do not like us any more than we like ourselves, or perhaps even less. A dramatic case illustrates the point: a woman was very uncomfortable about her prejudice against blacks, and her long series of sexual experiences with blacks, but was nonetheless distressed that T-group members (including several blacks) refused to deal with her apparently inconsistent attitudes and behaviour while strongly censoring both her openness and her as a person.

Lest the reader misunderstand the reason for the preceding discussion we go back to the research focus of this chapter. The point is that research on T-groups that is concerned with change may be sometimes confounded by the goals of the individual in the group. To test and confirm one's perception of self is a legitimate learning goal. But the testing and confirming may provide no motivation to change. Or, if perceptions are not confirmed, the person's defences may prevent change. In either case, research that is focused on change will have missed the mark, though the experience may have been meaningful for the individual.

Different strokes for different folks

The generalizations in the literature are also significant because – even if all or most members of any T-group need and
want to change – needs and wants vary. Thus some members
might want and need to be more assertive, while others might
tone down substantially. Others might be told they were quiet
or boisterous, but would choose not to change. And the same
T-group could serve all these individuals, although only a very
subtle research design could hope to isolate such diverse effects.

No wonder, then, that individual studies of T-groups have
generated results which vary widely. Part of this variance can
presumably be accounted for by the degree that needs differ.
Such divergence of individual needs is difficult to demonstrate
in any small group of subjects.

Consistently, research findings present fewer surprises when
they are guided by designs which conceive of the T-group as
moderating extremes in attitudes. Harrison (1971) develops
this concept in a revealing contrast of two concepts of the
T-group as moderating extremes of attitude. Thus a T-group
may be seen 'as the place where sharp edges are rubbed off
people'. Alternatively, the T-group may be seen as 'a place
where each individual is encouraged to explore and express the
latent and underdeveloped aspects' of self. In terms of experimental design, 'these both come to much the same thing'. The
two concepts are also equally useful for guiding research. Thus
Harrison (1971, p. 78) concludes expansively that 'It is noteworthy that there is not, to the author's knowledge, any study
which has used this method which has failed to show significant
results.' Harrison correctly assesses the literature, although
some exceptions do exist.[1]

Research must be subtle to isolate such diverse effects. In
turn, any generalizations drawn from research whose designs
do not conceive of the T-group as moderating extremes would
have to reflect dominant tendencies indeed to rise above the
welter of learnings going this way and that.

The point receives substantial support from research and

1. See Golembiewski, (1972, pp. 261–2).

experience that implies learning or change is most likely in 'balanced groups'. Balanced groups imply two conditions. T-groups should be so composed that each member can find substantial support from members with similar characteristics. They should also be composed so that each member can interact with a number of members with contrasting characteristics (Harrison, 1965). The underlying model is one of balance. It seeks to avoid:

* too much stress, as when an individual's preferred skills and values differ markedly from those of all or almost all other group members, which can so threaten or confuse an individual as to inhibit testing or normal interpersonal skills and values;
* too much 'success', when the individual's preferred skills and values are supported by most or all group members, which discourages self-analysis and searching for alternative skills or values;
* inadequate alternative models against which the individual can compare personal skills or values, and from which alternative skills or values can be selected;
* inadequate support for alternative behaviour or attitudes, as when most or all members of a T-group behave so as to restrict some member to their own image.

It is not yet certain which characteristics are most central for achieving contrast-*cum*-support, however, nor is it clear how these characteristics may be measured. Balanced groups have been composed of members who vary in their need to exercise power. Or such groups can be composed, half and half, of members who tend toward 'concrete thinking' and those who tend toward 'abstract thinking'. But much work remains to be done in this critical area.

Not everyone learns or changes equally

It may seem an elementary point, finally, but expectations about learning have to be limited by knowledge about the learner. This reasonable notion has little penetrated into most research designs, however, despite evidence of the importance of individual differences (Golembiewski and Munzenrider, 1975).[1] In marked contrast, in fact, a kind of homogeneity hypothesis has influenced most research on laboratory education: everyone can and should learn from such an experience. This is quite unrealistic.

The critical nature of the link between learner characteristics and degree of learning can be illustrated by two conditions. Firstly, evidence suggests that those persons learn or change most whose attitudes, values, and skills are initially furthest from the values of the laboratory approach.

The general failure to specify this variable can have profound effects on T-group research. Firstly, T-groups made up of members with attitudes similar to those of the laboratory approach will tend to have little impact on their members for obvious reasons. Interpreters of research results, however, may conclude that T-groups in general are ineffective.

Secondly, evidence suggests that the degree of a participant's involvement in a T-group is a critical determinant of how much he learns or changes. Often this important condition is not specified, which is convenient, but simplistic. For knowledge of actual self will no doubt be influenced by a participant's involvement in a T-group and the amount of feedback he receives.

Conclusion

This chapter ends as it began: with optimism that more is known than a few years ago, and with the realization of how much yet remains unknown. We have tried to provide three related kinds of useful detail:

* perspective on the complexity and subtlety of choice and change in interpersonal and intergroup relationships,
* some impression of the consequences of T-group experiences in general,
* some sense of the conditions that influence the consequences of a T-group for an individual.

1. An exception is a recently published study (Lennung and Ahlberg, 1975) in which the research specifically focused on change related to individual differences. The differences taken into account were genetic make-up, previous learning history and social situation.

10 Coping with the Transfer Gap

The focus of this book thus far has been on the internal dynamics of the T-group. However powerful the immediate experience, the prime value of laboratory education is what happens at home in the learner's everyday life. This chapter seeks to counterbalance the bias of earlier chapters towards viewing the T-group as internal and short-term. The dimensions of the 'transfer gap' – the relative difficulty of bridging the psychological space between training and home – are thus critical in determining the efficacy of laboratory education.[1]

The associated issues deal with the potency of laboratory education as a vehicle for planned social change. If the transfer gap cannot be effectively bridged, T-groups may be unproductive and even counterproductive. The inefficiency of transfer may just induce frustration. In the T-group, the learner has been to the top of the mountain, but has to come down again when he goes home. It is a very good rule-of-thumb that expectations should be raised only when there is some real possibility of attaining them. Personal and social chaos is the probable result of raising expectations without increasing actual achievement.

In counterbalancing the internal bias of this book, this chapter focuses on two questions associated with the 'Applications of Learning' dimension of Figure 7. These questions are:

Firstly, has a learner following a laboratory experience been able to help others learn at home, to help them learn how to learn?

Secondly, has a learner been able to change or modify

1. A convenient and comprehensive overview of the laboratory approach to organization development may be found in Friedlander and Brown, (1974).

aspects of his daily environment, at work, in the family, and so on? The specific approach to providing insight about transfer success or failure is via three facets of the transfer gap. The following sections deal with the following points:

* Home forces are sketched, showing how change and learning are the result of a complex field of forces in tension.
* Consideration is given to two models of learning or change, 'fade-out' and 'fade-in'.
* Attention is given to ways of reducing the transfer gap by designing learning systems other than T-groups in the laboratory approach.

This chapter, combined with the analysis in the preceding chapter, provides the basis for answering the major question concerning any learning technology: do the probable outcomes of the technology justify the risks?

Facilitators and inhibitors of transfer

Although T-group training does induce change in participants, research into the permanence of any changes and their transfer into other environments has yielded mixed results. On the one hand, there are dramatic illustrations to show that even substantial T-group learning was not carried into home settings (Argyris, 1965). On the other hand, studies establish that major transfer did occur, with learning retained over even extended periods (Golembiewski and Carrigan, 1973).

Diverse findings are perhaps to be expected at this early stage of research; they testify to the complex field of forces that can be disturbed by efforts to transfer T-group learning. Successful transfer depends on many conditions. Both practitioners and researchers can reasonably expect to proceed up assorted cul-de-sacs as they seek to make progress. Complicated and sometimes painful readjustments and reconceptualizations no doubt will be necessary, and it is even conceivable that the present learning technology will have to be scrapped.

Here we sketch a number of conditions concerning effective transfer, including both what we can be reasonably certain about, and what we still need to know.

It is easy to be intimidated by the unknown, but this chapter is optimistic as well as cautious. It seems likely (but hardly certain) that specifying variables will help increase the consistency of the results reported about transfer and permanency of changes. We would not expect that all or even most participants in any specific T-group would transfer learning into other areas of their life any more than we would expect participants to experience the same learnings to the same degree. Available research implies that transfer and permanence of learning are more likely under certain conditions.

Learner's status

Common wisdom is that status has an effect on transfer, but is uncertain of its exact nature. The higher a person's status in a system, goes one formulation, the more he becomes a member and defender of the establishment. Alternatively, the higher a person's status, the more resources available to influence and change that system.

The latter formulation seems to apply to transfer of T-group learning. To the degree that a person can influence or control an environment, so that person is likely to transfer T-group learning into it. For example, Miles (1965, p. 214) found that high rates of transfer of learning into schools by administrators[*] following a T-group experience were achieved by participants who had high status, as reflected by:

* high security (measured by length of tenure);
* high power (measured by the number of persons supervised);
* high autonomy from immediate superiors (measured by the length of the time between required reports).

Practice for transfer

Substantial evidence suggests that transfer of T-group learning into other contexts is more likely if the design of the experience emphasizes application of the training to home situations (Bunker and Knowles, 1967). Again, it would be surprising if it were otherwise.

This reasonable if tentative conclusion gets substantial

support from many studies which reflect the critical role of what may be called 'practice-for-transfer'. Consider the relatively common finding that T-group experiences do change the style in which people describe and analyse interpersonal problems. Even then the learner does not always see a clear connection between the new perceptions and how they can be translated into effective action. To put it otherwise, one critical component in the transfer gap is the discrepancy between insight and action.

Whether the conclusion is reasonable or not, however, T-group experiences usually devote little time and attention to how insight can lead to action at home. This is largely due to most T-groups being formed of relative or absolute strangers. Attention to home issues is thus difficult for multiple reasons. For example, strangers have only the T-group experience in common, and much retelling of history is necessary to explain home situations. These factors encourage reliance on learning designs that maximize the immediate impact of the T-group, which is easier to do than to reduce the transfer gap.

The home context

Research indicates that the properties of home contexts are important determinants of transfer success and failure.

The indefinite character of research on the point can be sketched in terms of two somewhat contradictory propositions. Firstly, up to some point, transfer seems to be more marked when the home context has different values from the laboratory. Second, beyond that point, the differences can become so great that transfer is lessened.

Clearly, transfer involves delicate fine-tuning. But we are better at finding examples of the need for fine-tuning than examples of successful fine-tuning. William Underwood provides a case-in-point: many of the T-group trainees in his firm were seen as having changed after returning to work following a T-group experience. But a number of them had changed in ways that were seen as reducing their effectiveness in the organization. He explains:

The experimental subjects were reported to show decreased effectiveness in the personal category in a substantial number of reports. An analysis of these changes reveals a heavy emotional loading in the nature of the change. It is speculated that these subjects were venting emotion to a greater degree than usual and to the observers, *operating in a culture which devalues such expression*, this behavior yielded a negative evaluation. (Underwood, 1965, p. 37).

The home context can wash out even substantial positive effects of training. That is to say, the context can encourage the learner to retain his learning, but to partition it off from his behaviour in that context. Failure to transfer learning is not apparently so much a matter of lost capacity as of suppression, resulting from hostile home attitudes. The evidence is anecdotal, but convincing. For example, Argyris (1965) observed such an effect about ten months after T-group training. Participants were still exercising their retained capacity for openness, but only selectively. They were open with other participants, but increasingly guarded in the bulk of their interactions.

You have to get it to transfer it

Another reasonable limit on the automatic nature of transfer is at once patent and often overlooked. Since individuals vary in their learning in a T-group, substantial differences in transfer are to be expected. Consistently, research implies that transfer is greater in direct proportion to a participant's degree of involvement in a T-group, the amount and quality of feedback he receives and his reactions to it (French, Sherwood, and Bradford, 1966). The duration of a T-group experience also seems directly related to the probability of transfer of learning (Bunker and Knowles, 1967): greater duration permits enhanced opportunities for involvement and feedback, as well as for direct attention to transfer.

The proposition seems reasonable enough, but few studies provide appropriate information. The consequence is a familiar one: the results of studies are difficult to interpret and evaluate. Existing studies tend to take the form: of X participants in a T-group, Y made changes in some home context after their training, which persisted for such-and-such a time. Such results make interpretation difficult, if they are not seriously misleading, when they say nothing about the specific qualities of a T-group and its members. It is simplistic to expect every T-group to have more-or-less uniform effects on all or most participants. As with any learning system, some T-groups are failures for all or many members, and hence no transfer should be expected. But much of the discussion of transfer neglects this reality.

Fade-out and intensification

The degree of transfer of learning can be described in three basic ways:

* Substantial learning may persist at home.
* Substantial learning may persist for only a short time at home, and then disappear, perhaps regressing beyond the pre-training level (called 'fade-out').
* It may appear initially that little transfer occurs, but transfer does appear and increases over a period of time (called 'intensification').

The last two cases are especially interesting in the way in which these two apparently contradictory learning curves contain a significant common lesson for increasing transfer.

A case of fade-out

Learning fade-out has been relatively common in the history of planned social change. We often think of learning as a step function. Thus some progress occurs, the learner stays on a plateau for a while as if assimilating learning, and then some back-sliding occurs. Regression, in this view, is inevitable in learning and a realistic goal is to achieve two steps forwards, and only one-and-a-half backwards.

The literature contains many examples of change efforts of this variety. At International Harvester, a training programme designed to induce specific changes in the attitudes and behaviour of foremen centred around the empathic understanding known as 'consideration' in the behavioural sciences. The design used temporary learning groups of people who were relative strangers, in that they did not work closely together. The programme seemed successful at first, but learning fade-out was extreme. No sooner had the foremen returned to work than changes due to training not only began to decline, but after a short period back at work the trained foremen actually scored lower on the target variables than a control group of untrained foremen. The foremen who retained their increases, significantly, worked for superiors who themselves scored high on the target attitudes. Gene W. Dalton (1970, p. 50) concludes:

> The other foremen (whose superiors did not place a high value on consideration) returned to a pattern very close to that of their chief. Daily interaction completely negated the effect of the training program. The foremen's ties had been interrupted only during the two week training period. Then they returned to a situation where the most significant relationship was with their own supervisors. No continuing new relationships had been established which would act to confirm and reinforce any attitude changes begun in the training program.

A case of intensification

The intensification effect is illustrated by a human relations training programme for supervisors (Hand, Richards, and Slocum, 1973), which utilized ninety-minute sessions in each of twenty-eight consecutive weeks in an effort to induce changes in some relatively specific supervisory attitudes and practices. Again, the learning groups were temporary, in which supervisors were to gain insight, knowledge, and skills that they were later to transfer to their permanent work-units. The other members of their work-units received no training.

Early evidence seemed to indicate that the training had failed: ninety days after the programme ended, self-reports revealed little change in both the trained supervisors and in a control group who received no training. Fifteen months later, however, the trained supervisors reported major changes in the direction expected, and supervisors in the control group reported significant deterioration on the same scales.

The pattern of change had two significant, interacting implications. Firstly the changes occurred in work-units that had previously been exposed to both consultative and autocratic supervisory styles. Secondly, the researchers concluded that it was unreasonable to expect immediate change in organizational systems that had developed over a period of years: any process of change requires powerful reinforcement, and reinforcement takes time. The researchers observe:

The need for a period of time to elapse before the *a priori* expectations for a human relations program take effect would suggest an ongoing process during which the organization's decisions need to reinforce the attitudes learned in the training program. With decisions reinforcing training, it might be speculated that attitude changes would more likely be exhibited. In this case, the impact of the training program, time, and management's decisions were not evident in attitudinal differences after 90 days, although changes did occur after 18 months. (Hand, Richards and Slocum, 1973, p. 192).

What were the reinforcers in this case? Apparently there was no conscious plan for reinforcement, but upper levels of management tended to direct salary increases and promotions towards those managers who reflected or adopted behaviours or attitudes sought by the training programme. Hand, Richards and Slocum (1973, p. 187) describe these conditions briefly:

The firm under study competes in a segment of the industry in which rapid technological change is occurring in both their products and their production processes. The executives of the firm selected the change program in the belief that the desired changes would be beneficial not only to the managers, but also to their subordinates.

Limitations of the stranger model

Examples of fade-out and intensification are common, and researchers came to appreciate a major common implication, namely, the limitations of the 'stranger model' of change. As in the two cases above, the stranger model creates *ad hoc* learning groups. These are composed of individuals who share only their immediate experience and some category similarities, such as all participants being at a similar managerial level. Such groups have no past or future. Their members are strangers before the training, and the groups cease to exist after training. Participants are to carry back any learning or insight to permanent groups, where few or no people have themselves experienced the training. The phases of the stranger model for inducing change look something like this:

Stranger model

1.
Key individuals, such as supervisors, have a learning experience as strangers or semi-strangers to develop some skills or attitudes, in a T-group, a human relations seminar, etc.

2.
Each key individual returns to his own work unit, to implement his learning.

3.
Change may occur, triggered by the key individual and adopted by others in his work unit.

The stranger model received a great deal of attention early on for various reasons: it is comfortably elitist, and consistent with common organizational notions about the roles of the leader and the led. It also seems economical: it proposes to train only certain key individuals, who are then 'seeded' until they achieve, presumably, a kind of social 'critical mass' sufficient to induce change involving more of an organization's members. Moreover, experiences in a group of strangers allowed for privacy, permitting learners to test behaviour that might seem unusual or even wildly improbable in a permanent work-group, and to do so in a temporary context whose participants had no prior history, no long-standing rivalries or conflicting ambitions, and no future.

These advantages of stranger experiences are real and powerful, but two kinds of evidence continued to accumulate. Thus learners still reported powerful experiences in T-groups. But they also reported that home applications were few and limited. Learners might report transfer of learning to relationships with wife or family. However, learners seldom reported changes at work. Or when changes did occur the delay in transfer implied the existence of dynamics that were not being taken into explicit enough account by the stranger model.

Accumulating evidence like this led to a growing emphasis on the 'family model' of change. It takes the following form:

Family model

1.	2.
A total natural-state 'family' – an entire work unit, for example – has a common learning experience, as in a T-group or in a team-building session.	Changes in the behaviour, values, and attitudes of individual members may occur. Changes in organization climate or style may occur, which induce and reinforce appropriate change by individual members.

The change in focus is truly profound. Overall, the family model highlights the long-run responsibility of the individual for the impact of his actions. As Richard Parlour (1971, p. 343) explains:

> The people in the organization have to live with what they do. It is true that in some ways people will be cautious in self-expression in such situations because of possible repercussions from the other group members who have the power to do harm. Each person also has a vested interest in making the organization successful and reducing the unnecessary obstacles to smooth cooperation resulting between the members. Reality cannot be well confronted without including the power factor . . .
> We cannot know a person until we see what he does in real-life situations where he must bear the responsibility for his actions.

The change in focus of the family model is also promoted by a number of major difficulties with the stranger model of learning. Let us look at initial learning in T-groups. Six themes will detail central problems of the stranger model in triggering transfer of learning or home change (Golembiewski, 1972). The focus is on T-group learning, as well as on transfer into some kind of work environment rather than into alternative contexts such as families.

Firstly, the stranger model assumes that personal insight can change organizational systems. Experience clearly demonstrates that the two are not linked in any simple way, however. Personal insight does allow some control over intellectual and emotional aspects of some issues, but one can have insight by the yard, and still have little or no control over the strategic variables necessary for organizational change. As Warren Bennis (1963, p. 138) notes:

It is not obvious that insight leads to sophistication in rearranging social systems or in making strategic organizational interventions. It seems therefore that the insight strategy ... is a questionable strategy. If anything, applied social science depends on the policy-makers controlling the relevant variables. Insight provides these as far as personal manipulation goes, but it is doubtful that it can lead directly to external manipulations of social systems.

Alexander Winn (1966, p. 78) adds an important counterpoint to Bennis' position. He asks rhetorically: '... how can one transfer the climate of trust, of emotional support and acceptance for what one is, from [a T-group] into a wider [organization that] more frequently than not, shares different values, different beliefs, norms, and expectations?' Insight does not suffice, clearly enough.

Indeed, insight without follow-up action can become frustrating: it only sharpens the sense of pain or loss, and deepens the sense of frustration.

Secondly, the relevance to work conditions of material discussed in stranger T-group experiences is not always clear and direct. For example, a here-and-now conflict in a stranger T-group might provide insight and perspective about a conflict an individual had back at the shop. The critical act is linking this to the situation at work. By definition, a stranger experience does not provide the same context for such a linkage as is available in a family group. The consequences can be very damaging. For example, Sheldon Davis (1968, p. 5) condemns some of the limitations inherent in stranger laboratory experiences:

Say a man has a good experience. He comes back to the job full of new values – and sits down in the same crummy atmosphere he left a week before. He may be changed, but his environment isn't. How can he practice confrontation with a boss and a secretary and colleagues who don't even know what it's all about? In a few weeks he's either completely dazed or has reverted, in self-defense, to the old ways.

Thirdly, experience suggests that a stranger experience might even complicate the subsequent raising of such an issue at work, which is the only place it can be resolved. This point applies in several senses. The stranger experience might dissipate feelings or reactions that could motivate action at work. It might only deepen despair about constructive action at work, as an individual experiences how much his here-and-now reactions are determined by the there-and-then issue.

Fourthly, a stranger experience is not related to familiar organizations, specific authority structures with their own histories, traditions, and personalities. This simplifies the analytical task of members of stranger T-groups, but at a cost. At the very least, its absence removes highly relevant factors. Moreover, changes would have to be tested with organizational authorities, who might have considerable influence on the individual's career.

At their worst, indeed, some normal T-group processes may produce unexpected results at home. Consider 'unfreezing' of the typical T-group, which is facilitated '. . . by removing the familiar props and customary social mechanisms, by violating the expectations of trainees, and by creating an ambiguous, unstructured situation for them of unclear goals and minimum cues' (Bass, 1967, p. 215). Bass is concerned that this aspect of the T-group technology may have serious consequences for some individuals, even as it facilitates learning for others. For example, Bass worries that some participants may lose confidence in the exercise of authority, while others may be less willing to serve authority figures. Since authority and its acceptance are important in organizations, sometimes even crucial, such consequences would be profound. Bass notes (1967, pp. 215–16):

In short, the 'destruction' of the customary authority structure in the T-group in order to promote exploration and change in the individual participants, coupled with an emphasis on the values of democracy and consensus, may produce, in some participants at least, sufficient anti-authoritarian leadership attitudes to reduce their contributions to the organization at times when such directive leadership is required.

Fifthly, it is extremely difficult to integrate T-group learning into a pre-existing work group or family. Organizational jobs or roles have their own demands and there is no guarantee that enhanced individual mental health and maturity will help meet all such demands. Consequently, as Bass concludes, training people 'to be better diagnosticians with greater tolerance and social awareness' is perhaps necessary but not sufficient for organization development.

Sixthly, stranger experiences do not provide the continuous reinforcement that is at least useful and perhaps necessary to transfer individual learning into organization contexts. Indeed, substantial frustration may set in as individuals fail to gain reinforcement at work, and they may have to 'negatively relearn' in order to get back in phase with organization norms.

Increasingly, the family model has been seen as a convenient way of reducing the transfer gap. There is no need to transfer any learning gained in a family setting, whatever other concerns it might trigger. The natural unit is both the context within which learning takes place, and the one where it will be implemented. The only drawback is that individuals are more inhibited and may do less extensive searching of self in a family setting. We need to develop different learning designs for family experiences, since much of the basic T-group technology rests on the security of relative strangers interacting in their own unique social system. A survey of such design developments now follows.

Alternative designs for family experiences

Inspired by the growing sense of the usefulness of family experiences, substantial attention in recent years has been devoted to the development of appropriate learning designs. In general, these family designs are spin-offs from the T-group. They seek to use processes – like feedback and disclosure –

that are central in T-group dynamics, but modify them to suit the family context. The three sections below each illustrate one class of the development of designs for family experiences.

The review here will be brief. Interested readers can consult several convenient sources for details of these and other designs, as well as for summaries of available research.[1] The fourth section will sketch some differences in the potency and the applicability of several designs for family experiences.

T-group variants

A number of designs following the family model have made use of T-group variants, such as the 'organizational training laboratories' used by Friedlander. His description of this variant design emphasizes the advantages of family experiences:

> . . . these training sessions deal with the intact work group as an integrated system into which is introduced procedural and inter-personal change, rather than a collection of strangers representing different organizations – or unrelated components of the same organization.

*

The organizational training laboratory is directed at helping the individual bridge the hazardous, yet critical transition from his trainee role to the 'real life' role of his back-home environment, and at preventing dissipation of the training effects. Since much of the discussion centers upon the relevant work problems which the group actually faces, and since the members of the training group are also the members of the organizational work group, ideally there is a perfect consolidation of the training and organizational membership roles. The back-home and the here-and-now are one and the same.

*

Research emphasis is not only upon behavioral change in the individual, but also upon change of the individual within his organizational context, and changes in the organizational context or organic system of which the individual is one interacting part. (Friedlander, 1967, p. 241).

Organizational training laboratories thus apply a T-group

1. See Golembiewski (1972), and French and Bell (1973).

orientation in the context of technical and personal relationships. This sounds easier than it is because all T-group variants seek to operate at several levels, which generates complexity if it does not create conflict between more-or-less irreconcilable objectives. At best, then, these kind of T-group variants are like simultaneously patting your head and rubbing your tummy. T-group variants blend the here-and-now focus of the T-group with an orientation towards there-and-then issues rooted in the common history of the family group. The there-and-then focus of personal history and psychodynamics is not central in organizational training laboratories but – just as in a T-group – such factors can become salient.

All of these elements of an organizational training laboratory get dramatic illustration in a narrative describing an intense episode in one of the earlier applications of T-group variants for a family group. The focus is on Bob, a team member who is 'drowning' in his responsibilities at work. Bob is so distant from his colleagues that communication is laboured and ineffective, and he shows many signs that productive work and even pleasant living are no longer really possible for him. Bob is describing to his colleagues how he came face-to-face with himself on a long solitary trip out to sea on a small boat. There he recognized his deep loneliness, and what it was doing to him:

'I stand up in the boat and stare into the darkness, then up to the sky. Something surges over me. I throw my arms open wide and scream into the darkness . . . I wait . . . listen . . . Nobody hears me.'

People were crying for the lonely old man. There was the look of peace on Bob's face and slowly, somehow, the loneliness was leaving. He looked young, strong.

Softly, I said 'Do you realize you've taken us with you? You've given us the privilege of being the first on your boat.'

People said, 'Thank you, Bob.' 'You're a poet.' 'You've got great courage.' 'I could listen to you all night.' 'I've never known what a wonderful person you are.'

Jim asked, 'How old are you, Bob?'

'Forty-nine,' Bob replied.

Jim exclaimed, 'Is that all! You've been acting like you're an old man – like your life's over, like your career with the company was finished. You've even looked old.'

Jack said, 'You're a young, powerful person, Bob. Look at yourself.'

Bob's smile was young. He seemed to be overwhelmed with the adulation of the group – with the love that came by letting people in. (Kuriloff and Atkins, 1966, p. 85).

Despite evidence that such T-group variants can facilitate change, some observers are cautious about using such designs for family groups. Or perhaps the word 'realistic' should be substituted for 'cautious'. In any case, these observers emphasize that it may be difficult for a group to live or work together after one or more of its members have 'let it all hang out' in a training session. Such cautious observers are also concerned that the spirit of T-group openness might lower usual constraints and defences, with pointless or even harmful consequences. Thus material might be introduced into a work context even though it is not relevant to work or, worse still, even though it might complicate future work relationships. The reader can imagine likely results should it be revealed, for example, that a team member's spouse is an alcoholic. If that seems too tame, let them contemplate one team member's discovery that a spouse is making it with another team member.

There is another side to these cautionary observations. It has to do with organizational constraints on openness rather than excessive openness if supervisors and subordinates are included in the same group-learning context. The problem is obvious, centring on whether or not subordinates will feel free enough to learn. Clearly no pat answers can be given. Both of us have been involved in variants on T-group experiences in which supervisor–subordinate relationships have seemed to make no difference. And we have been party to situations where they did. A decision to conduct such training ought not to be taken lightly. Organization managers would be well-advised against advocating family group training without clear understanding of the nature of the problems to be dealt with and equally clear understanding regarding the orientation of the trainer.

Team development designs[1]

A broad family of non-T-group designs has been developed to help family groups learn from their own experience, to improve on their own processes. The underlying rationale is a simple one, as is suggested by these linkages:

Human   Interpersonal   Organization
Inputs $\longrightarrow$ and Intergroup $\longrightarrow$ Outcomes
               Processes

Simply, since interpersonal and group processes mediate in significant ways between inputs and outcomes, the focus is on improving those intervening processes. 'Team development' or 'team-building' are the most common approaches to improving the processes that link individual inputs and collective outcomes.

Like T-groups, team-development places major attention on interpersonal and intergroup processes, and seeks to facilitate feedback and disclosure. Thus the following processes are central:

* *communication*, as in who talks to whom;
* *the roles and functions of different group members*: self-oriented behaviour, performance of task, or maintenance activities associated with preserving viable relations between members;
* *group problem-solving and decision-making*:
* *group norms and group growth*:
* *leadership and authority*, as in issues of who influences whom;
* *intergroup cooperation and competition.*

T-groups and team development differ in some significant regards, however.

Firstly, team-development is broader in focus than the T-group. Thus team-development deals with process *and* content, interaction *and* structure, relationships *and* technology, the personal here-and-now *as well as* the organizational there-and-then. This breadth is clearly shown by the following list of foci in team development:

1. See Margulies and Wallace (1973) for a more comprehensive discussion of team development designs.

* the *group task*, whose short-run demands may be very compelling or even overwhelming;
* *group maintenance*, which refers to the management of what team members do 'to and with each other' as they work on the common task, for a team '. . . needs to have a growing awareness of itself . . . of its constantly changing network of interactions and relationships, and of the need to maintain within itself relationships appropriate to the task' (Lippitt, 1969, p. 102);
* *individual needs* of team members, which influence how a team does its work, and whose relative satisfaction determines the individual's involvement and commitment to his team;
* *organization expectations* about team performance which may be expressed in terms of production standards, acceptable levels of quality, broad policies and procedures, etc;
* *relations with other groups*, which can be critical in at least three general cases:
  (a) where two or more teams work simultaneously on subsystems of some project or product which must be integrated;
  (b) when two or more teams perform sequential steps on some project or product, so that the work pace and quality of one team is dependent upon and/or directly influences another team or teams;
  (c) where two or more teams are related as seller/buyer or producer/consumer of some service, as in typical line-staff relationships.

Secondly, team-development designs are more narrowly-focused and goal-oriented than T-groups. Team-development emphasizes long-run breadth or scope; T-groups tend to stress depth of immediate relationships and emotionality. In team development, relationships between team members do get major attention but the prime focus is on how the team integrates its own work and how it links up with the other relevant socio-technical systems. The T-group has a strong *internal* bias, a focus on its own dynamics so strong that the rest of the world often becomes distant. This central contrast is very clear in Lippitt's (1969, pp. 107–13) list of the major goals of team development:

* an understanding of, and commitment to, common goals of the family team and of the broader organization of which it is a part;
* the integration of resources of as wide as possible a range of team members, so as to engage their contributions and also to increase their owning of and commitment to a team's goals or products;
* the ability and willingness to analyse and review team processes, so as to prevent the accumulation of unfinished business and to improve team effectiveness;
* trust and openness in communication and relationships;
* a strong sense of belonging to the team by its members.

Thirdly, team-development designs use a wide range of approaches tailored to the complexity and the specialization of different organizational contexts. Thus both T-groups and team-development are generically similar in that they collect information about group activities or relationships; feed such information back into the group system; and plan for action in response to feedback and reactions. Team-development designs can utilize such a full range of approaches to this three-step sequence:

* A team might periodically meet to plan action in answer to questions like: How are we doing? How can we do better?
* A team might engage in an 'action research' design, as by completing a questionnaire describing group and organization characteristics and having the survey results fed back to the team as a basis for possible remedial action.
* An outsider can interview members of the team, and report back impressions so as to increase efficiency and effectiveness of the team.
* A team might collect information and get feedback by arranging a 'mirror design', as when a marketing unit seeks information about how it is perceived by an important

customer, and uses the feedback to improve the relationship.

* A team could embark on such development programmes as those based on Blake's Managerial Grid (Blake and Mouton, 1968).

* Two or more teams could agree to engage in confrontation each providing information and feedback about how it perceives the other. These form the basis for planning of action by each team, or by both together.

A number of these designs can also be used in T-groups, as can the confrontation design discussed below, though they were developed for non-T-group family experiences, and are usually 'safer' than pure T-group designs. There are drawbacks in 'safety'. For example, using an outsider to collect data and report it back to a family team does provide safeguards for team members, but it also can make it easier for them to deny or reject any information reflected back to them.

Confrontation designs

Confrontation designs are both simple and useful in a wide variety of situations, including T-groups. Two kinds of confrontation designs will be described here, one briefly, the second at some length. At the interpersonal or dyadic level, various straightforward confrontation designs have proved useful. Two individuals having an unsatisfactory relationship, for example, might complete and then exchange three lists as a basis for confrontation:[1]

* *positive feedback list*: things one person values in his relationship with the other person;
* *'bug' list*: things one person dislikes or cannot tolerate in his relationship with the other person;
* *empathy list*: predictions by one person of what will appear on the positive feedback and 'bug' lists of the other person.

The lists then become the focus for analysis by the pair, aided by a third person. The procedure '. . . is highly structured but it is also foolproof' (Fordyce and Weil, 1971, p. 114).

1. A detailed treatment of interpersonal conflict resolution is provided by Filley (1975).

Group confrontation designs require greater elaboration. Basically, this class of designs seeks to meet the issue of transfer head-on, and to concentrate on groups in direct contrast to the individual focus of T-groups. Group confrontations attempt to capitalize on basic laboratory dynamics while doing what the T-group in large organizations sometimes does weakly or not at all.

Confrontation designs have similar aims to organizational applications of sensitivity training, but the two differ in critical ways. Although confrontation designs can vary widely in specifics, seven core features particularly distinguish them from learning designs using T-groups (Golembiewski, 1972, pp. 466–8).

One, group confrontation designs involve as participants individuals who are hierarchically and/or functionally involved in some common flow of work. They deal with a specific topic or problem, such as relations between line and staff. The learning sought therefore has direct application to the job. Sensitivity training, on the other hand, often takes place in groups composed of strangers. 'Cousin' T-groups might be composed of individuals from the same organization who do not work closely together, but it is only after such a first experience, if then, that relational learning is attempted in family groups. So, group confrontations are safer designs, they focus on a narrow range of work-related issues, and they stress intergroup as opposed to interpersonal issues.

Two, confrontation designs involve two or more organizational entities whose members have real, specific, and unresolved conflicts, e.g. labour and management. In this sense they are highly structured and content-oriented; T-groups are not.

Three, group confrontation designs involve the mutual development of images as a basis for attempting to highlight unresolved issues. Assume there are only two groups, Us and Them. The instructions to Us would be to develop three-dimensional Images based on these questions:

* How do we see Us in relation to Them?
* How do we think They see Us?
* How do We see Them?

The Them group would be given similar instructions. The 3-D images are prepared in private and written on large sheets of paper.

The act of developing a 3-D image, in effect, involves both feedback and disclosure. However, both processes are far more limited and controlled than in a T-group: they are written, and are hence more deliberate than those processes are likely to be in T-groups. Moreover, all 3-D images are tested in advance before they are communicated. Those doing the testing have a common stake in what is communicated, and they are thus able and motivated to control more daring members in ways that are not so obviously available in T-groups.

Four, confrontation designs provide for sharing 3-D images with participating groups, as the first step towards working through any relational problems. A consultant is present at each confrontation, and helps all parties to understand the elements in a 3-D image, to clarify, gives examples, and so on.

Five, confrontation designs assume that organizational problems often are caused by blockages in communication. The intent is that confrontations will free people to speak openly, and consequently set the stage for more authentic interaction and more effective problem-solving. Some objective dilemmas – such as a lack of money – cannot be resolved by confrontation designs, of course. In such cases, the best outcomes are greater clarity in communicating about such dilemmas, and greater willingness to collaborate in doing as much as conditions permit.

Six, confrontations are short affairs, lasting a matter of hours, perhaps a day or two at most. A typical stranger or family experience in a T-group lasts at least one week, and often two.

Seven, a confrontation design is seen as a springboard for organizational action. Since such a design is brief, however, real limits exist as to what can be accomplished. Participants are told to try to understand the 3-D images communicated to them, and to seek some areas of agreement where mutually beneficial accommodations might be made. There may often be some kind of follow-up, such as special-interest groups to work on issues that require deliberation and development.

Provision may also be made for reporting the results of a special-interest group to all participants so that they can be implemented.

In summary then these seven common features indicate that the results of confrontation designs do not have to be transferred or made relational. They are relational, for good or ill.

Research and experience suggest that confrontation designs have proved useful in a wide variety of organizational and inter-personal situations – their effects are both relatively immediate and long-lasting (Golembiewski and Blumberg, 1968, 1969).

Differences between family designs

All family designs are not equally strong or universally applicable, of course, but it is instructive to highlight two tentative findings in the literature, slim though it is. This is the case even though we have here illustrated only a few of of the possible family designs, and we have only scratched the surface of the two possible programmes of planned change. For broader perspectives on this latter point, consult Crowfoot and Chester (1974), and Van de Vall (1975). For alternative family designs, the contributions of Zand (1974), and Luke *et al.* (1973) illustrate the growing available literature relevant to theory and practice.

Potency of different family designs

One recent study compared the effects of four different designs, all applied to family groups in large organizations (Bowers, 1973). They found that different designs had effects that differed markedly enough to suggest some regular differences in potency. They compared the effects of four designs which were, in decreasing order of effectiveness:

* *Survey research* begins with a questionnaire asking about team and organization characteristics, and seeks to help a group '. . . move from a discussion of tabulated perceptions, through a cataloging of their implications, to commitment

to solutions to the problems identified and defined by the discussion' (Bowers, 1973, p. 24).

* *Interpersonal process consultation* is very similar to team development described above.
* *Task process consultation* '... begins by analysing a client unit's work-task situation *privately*, after extensive interviews concerning its objectives, potential resources, and the organizational forces blocking its progress' (Bowers, 1973, p. 25) and rests on extensive private contacts with the supervisor.
* *T-group training* – the group-oriented laboratory extensively described in earlier chapters.

Survey research, therefore, was the most effective and T-groups the least.

A significant intervening condition

The survey research approach was understandably the most efficient in inducing change at work, especially since it used a questionnaire which directed attention to a broad range of organizational characteristics. The other designs, especially T-group training, focus less on such organizational characteristics – hence their lesser effectiveness in inducing change at work, due to a greater transfer gap.

The summary conclusion should not however be taken entirely at face-value, however. It may more precisely be said to reflect the different potency of designs under a specific condition. As Bowers (1973, p. 41) notes, T-group training was applied at sites generally characterized by an '... organizational climate that is *becoming* harsher and more barren'. He concludes:

This may, in fact, explain the discrepancy between findings in the present study and findings reported elsewhere: it may be that laboratory-like, experiential learning is successful in organizations whose climate is, or is becoming, positive ... but unsuccessful in organizations whose superstructure is, or is becoming, more autocratic and punitive. (Bowers, 1973, p. 41).

A series of independent studies provides some support for Bowers's hypothesis. Broadly, the studies deal with two kinds of organization units, growth-oriented and stability-oriented, corresponding to the two types described by Bowers. Figure 10 characterizes the two kinds of organization units in detail.

A common learning design – variant T-groups featuring confrontations with superiors at several hierarchical levels – showed similar patterns but different levels of change in the two types of units, consistent with Bowers's hypothesis. As the researchers explained:

Specifically, the learning design was expected to induce similar patterns of change in interpersonal and intergroup relations in the two types of organization units, but greater magnitudes of change were expected in the Growth-Oriented Units.

The rationale for the expected difference in [level of] change can be illustrated briefly . . . Being 'safe' and not 'rocking the boat' would be more likely in Stability-Oriented Units, then . . . (Golembiewski and Carrigan, 1973, pp. 21–2).

A variety of data support this basic expectation, in essence and in detail.

A concluding note

A note of caution is appropriate, in conclusion. No technique is superior to the values that direct and condition its use. When all is said and done, group training rests upon a moral statement of the relationships that should exist between people and groups. A number of these values are stressed in earlier chapters. When this critical interdependence of technique and value is neglected, techniques are likely to be counterproductive, at least in the longer run.

Machiavellians as well as the over-eager and under-committed are hereby warned. Group training of the kind discussed here essentially implies a social order, and one that often differs fundamentally from the social order in much of everyone's life. Unless a realistic commitment exists to begin exploring the dimensions of this new and different social order, experimenting with group training is probably ill-advised. Beginning a programme of group training is rather like setting a tiger loose in the streets. One must be willing and able to cope

Figure 10 Two contrasting types of organization units

Growth-oriented units	Stability-oriented units
1. short organizational histories	1. several decades of organizational history
2. marked flexibility in policies and procedures	2. traditional policies and procedures
3. product lines that are new in markets that are sharply expanding	3. product lines that are aging in markets that are 'mature' and perhaps declining
4. profit opportunities are attractive	4. profit opportunities still good, but declining, and perhaps precipitously so
5. substantial growth in personnel and expanding opportunities for promotion	5. substantial reductions in personnel will occur, hopefully by attrition only, and opportunities for promotion are few
6. of apparently-growing present and future importance to parent corporation	6. traditionally the source of corporate leadership, but units may play lesser role in corporation of the future
7. look forward to continued growth	7. seek stability or even a gentle decline

with the consequences. Otherwise it is safer to keep the tiger caged, if one can, and if one is willing to accept the moral responsibility for the caging.

References

ALLEN, G. (1968), 'Hate therapy', *American Opinion*, March 1968, pp. 73–86.

AMERICAN PSYCHIATRIC ASSOCIATION (1970), *Encounter Groups and Psychiatry*, Washington, D.C.

ARGYRIS, C. (1962), *Interpersonal Competence and Organizational Effectiveness*, Dorsey Press, Homewood, Illinois.

ARGYRIS, C. (1964), 'T-groups for organizational effectiveness', *Harvard Business Review*, vol. 42, pp. 60–74.

ARGYRIS, C. (1965), 'Explorations in interpersonal competence – II', *Journal of Applied Behavioral Science*, vol. 1, pp. 255–69.

ARGYRIS, C. (1967), 'On the future of laboratory education', *Journal of Applied Behavioral Science*, vol. 3, pp. 163–83.

ARGYRIS, C. (1968), 'Conditions for competency acquisition and therapy', *Journal of Applied Behavioral Science*, vol. 4, pp. 147–77.

ARGYRIS, C. (1971), *Intervention Theory and Method*, Addison-Wesley, Reading, Massachusetts.

ASCH, S. E. (1960), 'Effects of group pressure upon the modification and distortion of judgements', in D. Cartwright and A. Zander (eds.), *Group Dynamics*, 2nd edition, Row Peterson, Evanston, Illinois.

BACK, K. W. (1972), *Beyond Words*, Russell Sage Foundation, New York.

BACK, K. W. (1973), 'The experiential group and society', *Journal of Applied Behavioral Science*, vol. 9, pp. 7–20.

BASS, B. M. (1967), 'The anarchist movement and the T-group', *Journal of Applied Behavioral Science*, vol. 3, pp. 211–27.

BENNIS, W. G. (1962), 'Goals and meta-goals of laboratory education', *Human Relations Training News*, vol. 6, no. 3, Fall 1962, pp. 1–4.

BENNIS, W. G. (1963), 'A new role for the behavioral sciences: effecting organizational change', *Administrative Science Quarterly*, vol. 8, pp. 165–75.

BENNIS, W. G., and SHEPARD, H. A. (1956), 'A theory of group development', *Human Relations*, vol. 9, pp. 415–37.

BENNIS, W., and SLATER, P. (1968), *The Temporary Society*, Harpers, New York.

BERNE, E. (1961), *Transactional Analysis in Psychotherapy*, Grove Press, New York.

BERNSTEIN, B. (1970), 'A social linguistic approach to socialization', in J. Gumperz and D. Hymes (eds.), *Direction in Social Linguistics*, Holt, Rinehart and Winston, New York.

BION, W. R. (1948), 'Experiences in groups', *Human Relations*, vol. 1, pp. 314–20 and 487–96.

BLAKE, R. R., and MOUTON, J. (1968), *Corporate Excellence through Grid Organization Development*, Gulf Publishing, Houston, Texas.

BLUMBERG, A., and GOLEMBIEWSKI, R. T. (1969), 'Laboratory goal attainment and the problem analysis questionnaire', *Journal of Applied Behavioral Science*, vol. 5, pp. 597–600.

BOWERS, D. B. (1973), 'OD techniques and their results in 23 organizations', *Journal of Applied Behavioral Science*, vol. 9, pp. 21–43.

BOYD, J. B., and ELLIS, J. D. (1962), *Findings of Research into Senior Management Seminars*, Hydro-Electric Power Commission of Ontario, Toronto.

BRADFORD, L. (1953), *Explorations in Human Relations Training*, National Training Laboratories Institute for Applied Behavioral Science, Arlington, Virginia.

BUCHANAN, P. C., and REISEL, J. (1972), 'Differentiating human relations laboratories', *Social Change*, vol. 2, no. 2, pp. 1–3.

BUNKER, D. R., and KNOWLES, E. S. (1967), 'Comparison of behavioral changes resulting from human relations training laboratories of different lengths', *Journal of Applied Behavioral Science*, vol. 3, pp. 505–23.

BURKE, R. L., and BENNIS, W. G. (1961), 'Changes in perceptions of self and others during human relations training', *Human Relations*, vol. 14, pp. 165–82.

BURTON, A. (ed.) (1969), *Encounter*, Josse-Bass, San Francisco.

CAMPBELL, J. P., and DUNNETTE, M. D. (1968), 'Effectiveness

of T-group experiences in managerial training and development',
Psychological Bulletin, vol. 70, pp. 73–104.

CHURCH, G., and CARNES, C. D. (1972), *The Pit: A Group
Encounter Defiled*, Outerbridge and Lazard, New York.

CLARK, J. V. (1962), 'Some troublesome dichotomies in human
relations training', *Human Relations Training News*, vol. 6,
no. 1, pp. 3–6.

COOPER, C. L. (1974), 'How psychologically dangerous are
T-groups and encounter groups?', *Human Relations*, vol. 28,
pp. 249–60.

CROWFOOT, J. E.' and CHESTER, M. A. (1974), 'Contemporary
perspectives on planned social change', *Journal of Applied
Behavioral Science*, vol. 10, pp. 278–303.

DALTON, G. W. (1970), 'Influence and organizational change',
in A. R. Negandhi and J. P. Schwitter (eds.), *Organizational
Behavior Models*, Comparative Administration Research
Institute, Kent, Ohio.

DAVIS, S. (1968), as quoted in J. Poppy, 'New era in industry:
it's OK to cry in the office', *Look*, 9 July 1968, pp. 64–76.

DUNNETTE, M. D., and CAMPBELL, J. P. (1968), 'Laboratory
education: impact on people and organizations, *Industrial
Relations*, vol. 8, pp. 1–27.

DYER, W. (1972), *The Sensitive Manipulator*, Brigham Young
University Press, Provo, Utah.

EGAN, G. (1970), *Encounter: Group Processes for Interpersonal
Growth*, Brooks/Cole, Belmont, California.

FILLEY, A. C. (1975), *Interpersonal Conflict Resolution*, Scott,
Foresman, Glenview, Illinois.

FORDYCE, J. K., and WEIL, R. (1971), *Managing with People*,
Addison-Wesley, Reading, Massachusetts.

FRENCH, W. L., and BELL, C. H., Jr (1973), *Organization
Development*, Prentice-Hall, Englewood Cliffs, New Jersey.

FRENCH, J. R. P., Jr, SHERWOOD, J. J., and BRADFORD,
D. L. (1966), 'Change in self-identity in a management training
conference', *Journal of Applied Behavioral Science*, vol. 2,
pp. 210–18.

FRIEDLANDER, F. (1967), 'The impact of organizational training
laboratories upon the effectiveness and interaction of ongoing
work groups', *Personnel Psychology*, vol. 20, pp. 289–307.

FRIEDLANDER, F., and BROWN, L. D. (1974), 'Organization development', *Annual Review of Psychology*, vol. 25, pp. 313–41.

GASSNER, S. M., GOLD, J., and SNADOWSKY, A. M. (1965), 'Changes in the phenomenal field as a result of human relations training', *Journal of Psychology*, vol. 58, pp. 33–41.

GIBB, J. R. (1964a), 'Climate for trust formation', in L. P. Bradford, J. R. Gibb, and K. D. Benne (eds.), *T-Group Theory and Laboratory Method*, John Wiley, New York.

GIBB, J. R. (1964b), 'Is help helpful?', *Association Forum*, February 1964, pp. 25–7.

GIBB, J. R. (1970), 'The effects of human relations training', in A. E. Bergin and S. L. Garfield (eds.), *Handbook of Psychotherapy and Behavior Change*, John Wiley, New York.

GIBB, J. R. (1974), 'The message from research', *The 1974 Handbook for Group Facilitators*, University Associates, La Jolle, California.

GIBB, J. R., and GIBB, L. (1969), 'Role freedom in a TORI group', in A. Burton (ed.), *Encounter*, Jossey-Bass, San Francisco.

GOLEMBIEWSKI, R. T. (1972), *Renewing Organizations*, Peacock, Itasca, Illinois.

GOLEMBIEWSKI, R. T., and BLUMBERG, A. (1968), 'The laboratory approach to organization change: confrontation design', *Academy of Management Journal*, vol. 2, pp. 199–210.

GOLEMBIEWSKI, R. T., and BLUMBERG, A. (1970), *Sensitivity Training and the Laboratory Approach*, Peacock, Itasca, Illinois.

GOLEMBIEWSKI, R. T., and BLUMBERG, A. (1969), 'Persistence of attitudinal changes induced by a confrontation design: a research note', *Academy of Management Journal*, vol. 12, pp. 309–18

GOLEMBIEWSKI, R. T., and CARRIGAN, S. B. (1973), 'Planned change through laboratory methods', *Training and Development Journal*, vol. 27, pp. 21–2.

GOLEMBIEWSKI, R. T., and MCCONKIE, M. (1975), 'The centrality of interpersonal trust in group processes', in C. L. Cooper (ed.), *Theories of Group Processes*, John Wiley, New York.

GOLEMBIEWSKI, R. T., and MUNZENRIDER, R. (1975), 'Social desirability as an intervening variable in interpreting OD effects', *Journal of Applied Behavioral Science*, vol. 11, pp. 317–32.

HAMPDEN-TURNER, C. (1966), 'An existential "learning theory" and the integration of T-group research', *Journal of Applied Behavioral Science*, vol. 2, pp. 367–86.

HAMPDEN-TURNER, C. (1970), *Radical Man*, Schenkman, Cambridge, Massachusetts.

HAND, H. H., RICHARDS, M. D., and SLOCUM, J. W., Jr (1973), 'Organizational climate and effectiveness of a human relations training program', *Academy of Management Journal*, vol. 16, pp. 185–95.

HARRIS, T. G. (1971), 'All the world's a box', *Psychology Today*, vol. 5, pp. 33–5.

HARRISON, R. (1962), 'Defenses and the need to know', *Human Relations Training News*, vol. 6, no. 4, pp. 1–4.

HARRISON, R. (1965), 'Group composition models for laboratory design', *Journal of Applied Behavioral Science*, vol. 1, pp. 408–32.

HARRISON, R. (1970), 'Choosing the depth of organizational intervention', *Journal of Applied Behavioral Science*, vol. 6, pp. 181–202.

HARRISON, R. (1971), 'Research on human relations training: design and interpretation', *Journal of Applied Behavioral Science*, vol. 7, pp. 71–85.

HAVELOCK, R. G., and HAVELOCK, M. C. (1973), *Training for Change Agents*, Institute for Social Research, University of Michigan, Ann Arbor.

HILGARD, E. R. (1948), *Theories of Learning*, Appleton-Century-Crofts, New York.

HOLLOMAN, C. R., and HENDRICK, H. W. (1972), 'Effect of sensitivity training on tolerance for dissonance', *Journal of Applied Behavioral Science*, vol. 8, pp. 174–87.

HOUSE, R. J. (1967), 'T-group education and leadership effectiveness: a review of the empiric literature and a critical evaluation', *Personnel Psychology*, vol. 20, pp. 1–32.

JANIS, I. L. (1971), 'Groupthink', *Psychology Today*, vol. 5, pp. 43–6 and 74–6.

JENKINS, D. H. (1962), 'Excerpts from a letter', *Human Relations Training News*, vol. 6, no. 1, pp. 2–3.

JENKINS, D. H. (1964), *Some Assumptions about Learning and Training*, unpublished manuscript, Temple University, Philadelphia.

JOURARD, G. M. (1971), *The Transparent Self*, revised edition, Van Nostrand Reinhold, New York.

KAHN, R. (1963), *Aspirations and Fulfillment: Themes for Studies of Group Relations*, unpublished Master's thesis, University of Michigan, Ann Arbor.

KLEIN, E. B., and ASTRACHAN, B. (1971), 'Learning in groups: a comparison of study groups and T-groups', *Journal of Applied Behavioral Science*, vol. 7, pp. 659–83.

KURILOFF, A. H., and ATKINS, S. (1966), 'T-group for a work team', *Journal of Applied Behavioral Science*, vol. 2, pp. 63–93.

LAKIN, M. (1969), 'Some ethical issues in sensitivity training', *American Psychologist*, vol. 24, pp. 923–8.

LENNUNG, S., and AHLBERG, A. (1975), 'The effects of laboratory training: a field experiment', *Journal of Applied Behavioral Science*, vol. 11, pp. 177–88.

LEWIN, K. (1951), *Field Theory in Social Science*, Harper, New York.

LIEBERMAN, M. A., YALOM, I. D., and MILES, M. B. (1973), *Encounter Groups: First Facts*, Basic Books, New York.

LIPPITT, G. L. (1969), *Organization Renewal*, Appleton-Century-Crofts, New York.

LIPPITT, G. L., and THIS, L. E. (1967), 'Leaders for laboratory training: selected guidelines for group trainers utilizing the laboratory method', *Training and Development Journal*, vol. 21, pp. 2–13.

LOMRANZ, J., LAKIN, M., and SCHIFFMAN, H. (1972), 'Variants of sensitivity training and encounter: diversity or fragmentation?', *Journal of Applied Behavioral Science*, vol. 8, pp. 399–420.

LUBIN, B., and EDDY, W. B. (1970), 'The laboratory training model: rationale, method, and some thoughts for the future', *International Journal of Group Psychotherapy*, vol. 20, pp. 305–39.

LUFT, J. (1969), *Of Human Interaction*, National Press Books, Palo Alto, California.

LUKE, R. A., JR, BLOCK, P., DAVEY, J. M., and AVERCH, V. R. (1973), 'A structural approach to organizational change', *Journal of Applied Behavioral Science*, vol. 9, pp. 611–35.

MANGHAM, I., and COOPER, C. L. (1969), 'The impact of T-groups on managerial behavior', *Journal of Management Studies*, vol. 6, pp. 53–72.

MARGULIES, N., and WALLACE, J. (1973), *Organizational Choice*, Scott, Foresman, Glenview, Illinois.

MEAD, W. (1973), 'Feedback – a "how-to" primer for T-group participants', in R. T. Golembiewski and A. Blumberg (eds.), *Sensitivity Training and the Laboratory Approach*, 2nd edition, Peacock, Itasca, Illinois.

MILES, M. B. (1965), 'Changes during and following laboratory training', *Journal of Applied Behavioral Science*, vol. 1, pp. 215–42.

MILGRAM, S. (1965), 'Some conditions of obedience and disobedience to authority', *Human Relations*, vol. 18, pp. 57–76.

MILL, C., and RITVO, M. (1969), 'Potentials and pitfalls of nonverbal techniques', *Human Relations Training News*, vol. 13, no. 1, pp. 1–3.

MILLS, T. M. (1964), *Group Transformation*, Prentice-Hall, Englewood Cliffs, New Jersey.

NATIONAL TRAINING LABORATORIES INSTITUTE (n.d.), *NTL Reading Book*, Arlington, Virginia.

NATIONAL TRAINING LABORATORIES INSTITUTE (1969), *Standards for the Use of the Laboratory Method*, Arlington, Virginia.

ODIORNE, G. (1963), 'The trouble with sensitivity training', *Training Directors Journal*, vol. 17, pp. 9–20.

PACKARD, V. (1972), *A Nation of Strangers*, David McKay, New York.

PARLOUR, R. R. (1971), 'Executive team training', *Academy of Management Journal*, vol. 14, pp. 341–65.

PERLS, F. (1969), *Gestalt Therapy Verbatim*, Real People Press, Lafayette, California.

PETERS, D. R. (1970), 'Self-ideal congruence as a function of human relations training', *Journal of Psychology*, vol. 64, pp. 199–207.

PFEIFFER, J. W., and JONES, J. E. (1969, 1970, 1971, 1973), *A Handbook of Structured Experiences for Human Relations Training*, Vols. 1, 2, 3, 4, University Associates, La Jolla, Calif.

RAFFERTY, M. (1970), 'Sensitivity training', *Syracuse Post-Standard*, Syracuse, New York, 20 April 1970.

ROGERS, C. R. (1961) 'The process equation of psychotherapy', *American Journal of Psychotherapy*, vol. 15, pp. 22–45.

ROGERS, C. R. (1970), *Carl Rogers on Encounter Groups*, Harper & Row, New York.

ROWAN, J. (1975), 'Encounter group research: no joy?', *Journal of Humanistic Psychology*, vol. 15, pp. 19–28.

RUBIN, I. (1967), 'The reduction of prejudice through laboratory training', *Journal of Applied Behavioral Science*, vol. 3, pp. 28–50.

SARASON, S. B. (1971), *The Culture of the School and the Problem of Change*, Allyn and Bacon, Boston, Massachusetts.

SCHUTZ, W. C. (1967), *Joy*, Grove Press, New York; Penguin, 1973.

SCHUTZ, W. C. (1974), 'Not encounter and certainly not facts', *The 1974 Handbook for Group Facilitators*, University Associates, La Jolla, California.

SCHUTZ, W. C., and ALLEN, V. L. (1966), 'The effects of a T-group laboratory on interpersonal behavior', *Journal of Applied Behavioral Science*, vol. 2, pp. 265–86.

SKINNER, B. F. (1971a), *Beyond Freedom and Dignity*, Alfred Knopf, New York; Penguin, 1973.

SKINNER, B. F. (1971b), 'Beyond freedom and dignity', *Psychology Today*, vol. 5, pp. 37–80.

SKOUSEN, W. C. (1967), 'Chief, watch out for those T-group promoters', *Law and Order Magazine*, November, 1967, pp. 10–12.

SMITH, P. B. (1975), 'Are there adverse effects of training?', *Journal of Humanistic Psychology*, vol. 15 pp. 29–47.

SOAR, R. (1966), *An Integrative Approach to Classroom Learning*, Temple University, Philadelphia.

SOLOMON, L. N., and BERZON, B. (eds.) (1972), *New Perspectives on Encounter Groups*, Jossey-Bass, San Francisco.

STANFORD, G. (1972), 'Openness as manipulation', *Social Change*, vol. 2, no. 3, pp. 1–2.

STEELE, F. (1975), *The Open Organization*, Addison-Wesley, Reading, Massachusetts.

TANNENBAUM, R., WESCHLER, I. R., and MASZARIK, F. (1961), *Leadership and Organization*, McGraw-Hill, New York.

TODD, R. (1971), 'Notes on corporate man', *Atlantic*, vol. 228, pp. 83–94.

UNDERWOOD, W. (1965), 'Evaluation of a laboratory method of training', *Training and Development Journal*, January 1965, vol. 19, pp. 34–40.

VAN DE VALL, M. (1975), 'Utilization and methodology of applied social research', *Journal of Applied Behavioral Science*, vol. 11, pp. 14–38.

VAN HORNE, H. (1970), *Philadelphia Inquirer*, 23 July 1970.

WEICK, K. (1969), *The Social Psychology of Organizing*, Addison-Wesley, Reading, Massachusetts.

WINN, A. (1966), 'Social change in industry: from insight to implementation', *Journal of Applied Behavioral Science*, vol. 2, pp. 120–84.

WINN, A. (1969), 'The laboratory approach to organization development: a tentative model of planned change', *Journal of Management Studies*, vol. 6, pp. 155–66.

YALOM, I. D. (1970), *The Theory and Practice of Group Psychotherapy*, Basic Books, New York.

YALOM, I. D., and LIEBERMAN, M. A. (1971), 'A study of encounter group casualties', *Archives of General Psychiatry*, vol. 25, pp. 16–30.

ZAND, D. E. (1974), 'Collateral organization: a new change strategy', *Journal of Applied Behavioral Science*, vol. 10, pp. 29–52.

Acknowledgements

Thanks are due to the following for permission to
reproduce copyright material:
Extracts from *Encounter Groups* by Morton A. Lieberman,
Irvin D. Yalom and Matthew B. Miles, Basic Books, Inc.
Extract from Syracuse *Post-Standare*, Los Angeles
Times Syndicate.

Index